"Russ Ramsey writes from his own inc̲.̲.̲.̲.̲ ̲.̲.̲.̲ ̲ ̲.̲.̲.̲ disease in real time. I was quickly caught up in the journey with him and felt like I became friends with him and the fascinating people he meets along the way. As a therapist who frequently references and recommends books, I moved this to the top of my list for many of the hard issues that we all face. Russ is vulnerable and honest about the deepest questions of life and leaves us with a peace that makes the unanswerable questions much less important. Russ combines Lewis's *A Grief Observed*, Keller's *The Meaning of Marriage*, and Kübler-Ross's *On Death and Dying* in one place and gives us the head and heart knowledge for trials that we all are familiar with. I'm proud to say that Russ is as real in his roles as my pastor and friend as he is in this book."

Kaka Ray, LMFT, trauma specialist

"Russ Ramsey has written a memoir that's as much about you as it is about him, because it's inviting and true to the human experience. His honest vulnerability and literary prose aren't simply talents, but offerings to God that beckon us to worship alongside him. This book is a gift."

Bethany Jenkins, director of The Gospel Coalition's Every Square Inch

"My word, Russ Ramsey has done a beautiful thing here. It takes absolute courage to walk through trauma and affliction and then return to it for the sake of others' healing. This book will be one you treasure, return to, and know just the right time to give to your friends."

Annie F. Downs, bestselling author of *Looking for Lovely* and *Let's All Be Brave*

"If you're not in the midst of struggle, one of these days you will be. That's why you need to read this book. By letting the reader into his struggles in a winsome and honest way, Russ Ramsey shows us how not to waste our own suffering."

Jonathan Rogers, author and meniscus surgery survivor

"Russ Ramsey is a rare bird—a pastor who's written a beautiful and honest account of his own suffering. Because he tells the whole story with truthful words, his book is an affirming balm, a call to hope, and a help through stages of affliction for anyone who reads it. The afterword written by his spouse, Lisa Ramsey, is a wonderful bonus!"

Andi Ashworth and Charlie Peacock, cofounders, Art House America

"*Struck* is Russ Ramsey's raw, unflinching look at what it means to be a person of faith in the midst of physical suffering. Doctors should read this book to better understand their patients. Nurses should read this book as a reminder to leave 'trail magic' for the weary. But this book isn't just for those who work in hospitals. To those whose lives or loved ones have been struck by pain, trauma, or heartbreak, this book speaks boldly about grief and the recovery process. Russ offers no silver linings. Instead, he offers the truth."

Claire Gibson, freelance writer, novelist

"In the spirit of C. S. Lewis's *A Grief Observed*, Russ has done us all a great service by chronicling his own journey into the darkness of grief and death and mortality. I'm so glad he recovered and came back from such a place to tell us this story—which is not so much about brokenness, but healing. This book has already been a comfort to me, and I have no doubt that it will be a comfort to many."

Andrew Peterson, singer/songwriter, author, proprietor of The Rabbit Room

"Russ has a way of articulating the complex intersection of faith and suffering that is profound yet approachable. In sharing this honest and beautifully written account of his own life-and-death experience, he succeeds in upholding both the mystery and confidence of the gospel, compelling us to take a closer look at a God who is as kind as he is sovereign."

Amanda Bible Williams, coauthor of *She Reads Truth*

"For anyone who is going through a season of affliction or is walking beside someone who is suffering, *Struck*, Russ Ramsey's personal account of his battle with a failing heart and his fight to survive, is a welcome source of encouragement and support. *Struck* will ignite your faith, strengthen your will, and give you hope for the future."

Eric Close, actor, *American Sniper, Nashville, Without a Trace*

"Russ Ramsey's *Struck* is a refreshing and honest take on the emotional and spiritual impact of physical struggle. There is no way to prepare for something like trauma. As someone who has been through it, Russ's words helped me to realize the things I felt while I was going through my own season of affliction."

Kris Allen, singer/songwriter, winner of *American Idol* Season 8

STRUCK

ONE CHRISTIAN'S REFLECTIONS
ON ENCOUNTERING DEATH

RUSS RAMSEY

Foreword by
SCOTT SAULS

IVP Books

An imprint of InterVarsity Press
Downers Grove, Illinois

InterVarsity Press
P.O. Box 1400, Downers Grove, IL 60515-1426
ivpress.com
email@ivpress.com

InterVarsity Press® is the book-publishing division of InterVarsity Christian Fellowship/USA®, a movement of students and faculty active on campus at hundreds of universities, colleges, and schools of nursing in the United States of America, and a member movement of the International Fellowship of Evangelical Students. For information about local and regional activities, visit intervarsity.org.

Scripture quotations, unless otherwise noted, are from The Holy Bible, English Standard Version, copyright © 2001 by Crossway Bibles, a division of Good News Publishers. Used by permission. All rights reserved.

While any stories in this book are true, some names and identifying information may have been changed to protect the privacy of individuals.

Cover design: Cindy Kiple
Interior design: Jeanna Wiggins
Images: © mariakraynova/iStockphoto

ISBN 978-0-8308-4494-4 (print)
ISBN 978-0-8308-9227-3 (digital)

Printed in the United States of America ∞

Library of Congress Cataloging-in-Publication Data
Names: Ramsey, Russ, 1973- author.
Title: Struck : one Christian's reflections on encountering death / Russ
  Ramsey ; foreword by Scott Sauls.
Description: Downers Grove : InterVarsity Press, 2017. | Includes
  bibliographical references.
Identifiers: LCCN 2016046957 (print) | LCCN 2016052035 (ebook) | ISBN
  9780830844944 (pbk. : alk. paper) | ISBN 9780830892273 (eBook)
Subjects: LCSH: Death--Religious aspects--Christianity. | Consolation.
Classification: LCC BV4905.3 .R37 2017 (print) | LCC BV4905.3 (ebook) | DDC
  248.8/6--dc23
LC record available at https://lccn.loc.gov/2016046957

P	21	20	19	18	17	16	15	14	13	12	11	10	9	8	7	6	5	4	3	2	1
Y	35	34	33	32	31	30	29	28	27	26	25	24	23	22	21	20	19	18	17		

For Mom and Dad, who fostered

the sort of faith that prized honesty

and left room for rough edges

In memory of

Barbara Ambrose and Ben Ellis

CONTENTS

FOREWORD

Scott Sauls

Reflecting on the future of the human race, Anne Lamott said candidly: "A hundred years from now? All new people."

I've always liked reading Anne Lamott for the same reason I like reading Russ Ramsey—because she cuts to the chase and, raw and unfiltered, tells the truth about life. And the truth about life is, at least for now, that it's temporary, fleeting, and fading, like a vapor. Because the current mortality rate is one person per every one person, none of us get to ride off into the sunset. At least it doesn't seem that way.

But for those whose personal stories are anchored in the story of Jesus, the threat of death is not a cause for despair. To be sure, it is a cause for momentary grief and sorrow and weeping, but attentive hearts also know that death is a prequel to paradise. The Bridegroom and the garden-city of God await, ready to catch us on the other side with the promise of no more death, mourning, crying, or pain (Revelation 21:1-5; 22:1-3).

In the end, death will lose its sting. Because Jesus is risen, we, too, will rise with renewed bodies and perfected hearts, minds, and motives. If we can imagine it (and even if we can't), every single day will be better than the day before. The "aging process" will no longer be marked by getting older and weaker, but younger and stronger, for infinite days.

This future vision, anchored and secured and irrevocably etched into the pages of Scripture, presents us with a hope that can carry us "through many dangers, toils, and snares." Its promise is that for every believer, the worst-case future scenario is resurrection and everlasting life in Jesus. Yes, in the end, that's as bad as it can possibly get for us in Jesus—uninterrupted, unhindered, perpetual bliss in the garden-city of God, with a tree in its center that is there for the healing of the nations. The empty tomb affirms that all these things are, and forever will be, trustworthy and true.

But what about now? What about the in-between time—these broken, never-predictable, wild, sorrow-filled, out-of-our-control, afflicted, fallen days in which we live? These are the days that bear hopeful glimpses and shadows of the world to come, but they are also the days that are, as Job the sufferer reminds us, numbered and hard. It's the numbered and hard days that make me thankful for authors like Russ Ramsey, and especially for this masterpiece that Russ, inspired by his writer-hero Annie Dillard, calls *Struck*. I need the story that Russ tells in these pages, and I need it in the way that he tells it.

Like Russ, I am a pastor whose job it is to help others through their numbered and hard days. Like Russ, I am also a jar of clay, a finite and fallen man, restless and frail, foolish and vulnerable, self-doubting and sometimes doubting of God. Like Russ, I have been anxious and depressed. Like Russ, I have doubted my calling and been through a vocational crisis. Like Russ, I have questioned the meaning of life and begged God to end it all. Like Russ, I have contemplated the inevitability of my own death. Like Russ, I have been involuntarily "lifted up" by the Creator who, as C. S. Lewis faithfully reminds us, is always good but never safe—and have been *struck* by him.

It is from this place of affliction, this place of being struck, that my heart (and yours?) becomes most receptive and most consciously needful of a story like the one that you now hold in your hands. The events about which Russ writes are not unique, because every person experiences grief and loss and brushes with death. And yet, there is an utter and uncommon uniqueness in the way that he tells this common story, because in the telling he offers us a new set of eyes and a glimpse of an inner life that is shaped by the world to come. He helps us, as N. T. Wright would say, to imagine God's future into our present sorrows and losses, and in the imagining—in finding our place in the story that is trustworthy and true—find truth, beauty, meaning, and hope.

In the beautiful telling of his own brush with death and the process of recovery, Russ shows us, in a most moving and lovely and hopeful fashion, what it means to find joy in the sorrow, beauty in the ashes, light in the darkness, intimacy in the fear, love in the losses, water in the wilderness, music in the sorrow, and yes, even life in the dying.

Russ, thank you for telling us the truth about life. Thank you for telling the truth in a most tender way. You are my friend and colleague, but you are also much more than this. You are a man who, in a most artful and thoughtful and heartfelt fashion, helps me see Jesus. May God give us all eyes to see as you do.

I had been my whole life a bell,
and never knew it until at that
moment I was lifted and struck.

ANNIE DILLARD

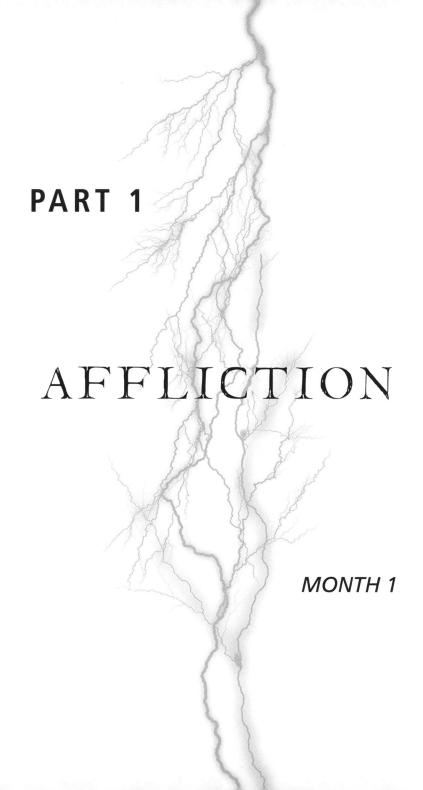

PART 1

AFFLICTION

MONTH 1

CHAPTER 1

LEARNING TO SEE

Affliction and Faith

*God whispers to us in our pleasures,
speaks in our conscience, but shouts in our pain:
it is his megaphone to rouse a deaf world.*

C. S. LEWIS

When my doctor told me I was dying, I came alive.

Three days before my fortieth birthday I was admitted to the emergency room. A bacterial infection had destroyed my mitral valve and I was in the early stages of heart failure.

That day and the two years that followed are the setting for this book. They are the setting, but they are not the subject. This is a book about what happens when affliction and faith collide.

I am a husband, father of four, pastor, and author living in the greatest "big small town" in America—Nashville, Tennessee. I lead a simple life. I get up early for work. I am rarely awake past 11:00 p.m. My wife and I go to bed tired. I have never dug a well in Africa or jumped out of an airplane. I am suspicious of people who use the word "epic" to describe their desired life. I am a simple man, and I do not presume that my story of affliction is all that unusual.

But it is not the uncommon parts of our suffering I am drawn to write about. I want to explore the common experiences afflicted people share—the onset of a sense of frailty, the fear, the grief, the humor, the routines, the new ways of relating to people who love us and are afraid for us and for themselves.

I have committed myself to the work of paying as much attention as I can to the medical, spiritual, relational, emotional, pharmaceutical, and physical experiences of this journey my failing heart has set me on. I have asked a lot of questions and taken a lot of notes and used them to write the chapters that make up this book.

Affliction awakens us to things we might not have seen otherwise. When I first learned of the severity of my condition I felt afraid, of course. But the prevailing sensation wasn't fear. It was wonder—curiosity, even exhilaration. I felt that I was at the beginning of a great adventure—one I instinctively did not want to miss. I have discovered that many in my position have felt the same way.

I want to interrogate my affliction. What happens when a person stands at the edge of their mortality and looks out into the eternal? What happens when a doctor tells a man he is dying? If that person believes in God (which I do), what will become of his faith? Will the spiritual premises he trusted as dependable foundations all those years earlier suddenly fail? Will he require certain personal outcomes in order for his faith to hold? And if so, is that even faith? Or is that nothing more than a house of cards too easily toppled by the winds of suffering?

I do not want simply to endure my affliction. I want to experience it—to receive it as an adventure and follow it to its end. I find the whole business fascinating. Knowing that I come to this season having seen the world only through the eyes of the well, I ask God to help me see whatever this struggle might reveal.

~~~

There is nothing automatic about learning to see with new eyes. In the early 1700s, doctors in the West discovered how to remove cataracts from the eyes of blind patients, giving them the ability to see. Annie Dillard, in her Pulitzer Prize–winning *Pilgrim at Tinker Creek*, wrote about what the experience of seeing for the first time was like for these people, many of whom had been blind since birth. One might presume the sensation would have been like someone turning on a light in a dark room—bringing clarity and information to an otherwise bewildering existence. But for many of these newly sighted people, who had already learned how to navigate the world through their other senses, the sudden ability to see was what confused them.

For the majority of patients, concepts like depth, size, shape, and space were nearly impossible to grasp. Dillard wrote, "For the newly sighted, vision is pure sensation unencumbered by meaning."[1] These patients had no categories for what they were seeing, and this was more than many of them could bear. Many became depressed because when they gained the ability to see, they lost the world as they knew it. Vision became a new form of blindness.

In response to their frustration, some simply refused to use their eyes. One doctor said of his patient, "Her unfortunate father, who had hoped for so much from this operation, wrote that his daughter carefully shuts her eyes whenever she wishes to go about the house, especially when she comes to a staircase, and she is never happier or more at ease than when, by closing her eyelids, she relapses into her former state of total blindness."[2]

For those who did not refuse their new sight, they had to learn how to use it. One man "practiced his vision in a strange fashion; thus he takes off one of his boots, throws it some way off in front of him, and then attempts to gauge the distance at which it lies; he takes a few steps toward the boot and tries to grasp it; on failing to reach it, he moves on a step or two and gropes for the boot until he finally gets hold of it."[3]

For those who practiced using their new eyes, the world they learned to see was filled with wonder. One twenty-two-year-old was so overwhelmed by the world's brightness that she kept her eyes shut tight for two weeks following her surgery. When at last she gathered the courage to open them "she did not recognize any objects, but the more she directed her gaze upon everything about her, the more it could be seen how an expression of gratification and astonishment overspread her features; she repeatedly exclaimed: 'Oh God! How beautiful!'"[4]

I want to know those moments when confusion gives way to beauty and wonder. I believe moments like these are bound to come for me in this season of affliction, if I look for them. When one such moment happened for Annie Dillard herself, she said, "I had been my whole life a bell, and never knew it until at that moment I was lifted and struck."[5]

For my whole life I have seen the world through the eyes of the well. This is all I have ever known. But now, I have been lifted and struck, and I want to hear what resounds in me. Though I may stumble for a time like a man reaching for his boot, I want to learn to see the world through the eyes of affliction.

This will be a challenge because I see this world and my place in it through the lens of what I already know. I can't help it. A dog is a dog and a pear is a pear. I can't see "Eden before Adam gave names."⁶ But affliction has the power, I believe, to quiet the voices in my head that think they already know everything. Seeing through my suffering won't show me a new world. Rather, it will show me more of the world I think I already know.

Affliction is bound to find us, and when it does whatever faith we profess, along with all its convictions regarding the meaning of this life and the next, is tested. Some affliction comes suddenly and lasts only a moment. Other affliction comes and takes us out of this world. Often though, affliction grabs us like an unsuspected wave and tosses us around in its currents for a season before washing us back up onto our familiar shores.

What then? Do we thank our lucky stars that we survived and try to return to the life we knew before any of this happened? Is that even an option? And if so, at what cost?

Affliction shapes our lives. It comes for us all—in our own personal distress or in the sufferings of those we love. It has come for me, and I know it will come again. The least I can do is pay attention.

I do not wish to waste my pain.

CHAPTER 2

STRUCK

The Onset of Affliction

*What was wonderful about childhood is that
anything in it was a wonder. It was not merely a
world full of miracles; it was a miraculous world.*

G. K. CHESTERTON

I was fifteen when our dirt road drifted shut. Everything
was draped in a blanket of shimmering white. I layered up and
headed outside. The air was bitterly cold—the dry kind that froze
the inside of my nose when I took a breath. The Indiana coun-
tryside was still. The sound my boots made as I crunched through
the surface of the snow echoed as though I were in an empty
concert hall.

I stood in the middle of my street, awed by how untouched my
world now appeared. This corner of creation onto which I had been
writing my existence with the black tread of bicycle tires suddenly
looked like a blank page, and I wanted to write all over it. I was old

enough to have taken a philosophical interest in the world but young enough to still approach it like a child; every tree I came upon was now an existential wonder I had to decide whether or not to climb.

The towering blue spruce at the end of our driveway sagged under the weight of the snow that had gathered on the end of its boughs. I saw something in the tree that told me I was not alone. There amid the alternating layers of bluish green and white sat a gray-speckled dove. I crept toward it, and though I could see its eyes, it did not fly away. It wasn't until I was only a few feet from it that I realized the little bird was dead, frozen solid where it had nestled in.

This was a sacred find because death was new to me, and I was curious. My exposure to mortality was limited to only a couple of memories. The first was of my father grieving several years earlier. He had just hung up the phone in our living room when I saw his shoulders begin to heave up and down. It was a kind of movement I had never seen him make before. He leaned forward like he wanted to tuck himself into a ball, and then he burst into sobs. Though I was only a few feet away from him, I remember how far he seemed from the rest of us as he wept. I would not have been more startled if he had stood up and danced around the living room like Fred Astaire. I was mesmerized. After he caught his breath, he managed to tell us that one of our neighbors, a farmer we all knew and loved, had just taken his own life. Though I couldn't express it at the time, my surprise at the sight of my father shaking from grief made me wonder what else I did not know about him, or of this world of ours.

And I remembered when my dog, Dusty, was hit by a car. After she was struck, she ran over to me and collapsed in my lap. I watched the light go out of her eyes. I was only nine when she died in my arms, and I wept and wept. Between Dusty's tragic end and my father's grief, I knew death was out there. And I instinctively knew this business of mortality was a problem no one wanted.

From my earliest encounters with the reality of death, I felt that it did not belong here. But I didn't know it well. My experience with it was like a world draped in snow; my tracks revealed I had never ventured far from the safety of home.

I picked up the little bird and held it in my gloved hands. It weighed next to nothing, as though it was hollow. As I studied the creature, a breeze came and ruffled its feathers, startling me into thinking it had snapped back to life. I almost dropped it in terror. Then I began to wonder, *what if this little bird came back to life?* What if it stood and stretched and flew away right then and there, right from the palms of my hands, off to God knows where?

Earlier that year I had become a Christian and had begun reading the Bible. Looking at the little creature, I remembered how the Bible talked about birds. God cares for the birds of the field, Jesus taught his disciples.[1] I thought that if God knew the number of hairs on my head, then he must surely know the number of feathers covering the dove in my hand.[2] I thought about how the Psalms tell us we are fearfully and wonderfully made;[3] how the earth is the Lord's and the fullness thereof.[4] If this was all true, then this was God's bird. He made it. He was there when it poked its little beak out of its little shell. He aligned its genetic makeup to produce feathers. He gave it instincts to find food. He gave it the proportions for flight. And he numbered its days—a number now expired.

I found myself caring for the little creature, even grieving—conjuring whatever sorrow I could. I was struck by the thought that God somehow loved this little lifeless bird in ways I could not comprehend. Such thoughts were new to me then, but present nonetheless.

I decided I would pray.

It started as a prayer of thanks for the wonder of creation and for God's attention to the tiniest details. Before I knew it I was praying for the bird itself. Like a priest presenting his offering to the Lord, I raised the dove up in my hands and prayed, "God of all Creation, you gave this bird life, and you have cared for it all of its days. Now it is dead. But if you wanted, you could bring it back to life. I know you could. It wouldn't take much. Just a word. Not even that.[5] So if it is your will, I pray that you would raise this little creature from the dead and give it new life."

Then, through the vapors of my own breathing, I stared at the bird in my hands and waited. What happened next changed my life. I felt like a bell that had been lifted and struck, and I can still hear the sound.

What results are we comfortable with here? Would it be acceptable if I testified that the bird came back to life—if I said it stood, unfurled its tiny wings, and took off into the crystal-clear blue? Would anyone believe me? Could they? *Should* they? How fantastic of a tale can I cantilever out over our common experience before it no longer holds? Can we speak of resurrection, of living after dying, and still be taken seriously?

Not only do I think I can, I believe I must. I am, after all, a Christian.

Christian people have always believed in the resurrection of the dead—not only in Jesus' resurrection but also in their own. In fact, there is no orthodox Christianity without it. Jesus taught his followers to believe in resurrection when he said, "Everyone who looks on the Son and believes in him should have eternal life, and I will raise him up on the last day."[6]

The trouble with talking about resurrection is that no matter who is having that conversation, they are speculating. There is nothing for it. We who have not yet died cannot hold any belief about what happens after we die except by faith. For some, that faith claim says that this life is all there is. When we die, we cease to exist. Religious people, on the other hand, believe there is some sort of life after death. I belong to that group, and I have reasons for believing as I do—reasons on which I have staked my entire life.

That doesn't change the fact that this remains a matter of faith. I recognize this. Still, I believe in resurrection—in the historical resurrection of Jesus of Nazareth and in the coming resurrection of those who trust in him.[7] I believe in this not primarily for how it addresses what happens to a person when they die, but for how it addresses a dying world. I believe in resurrection because when I look at the wonder of creation and the horrors of evil, I see a world groaning for healing, fighting for life, grieving over mortality.[8] I see how every longing to be loved is a longing that could be more deeply satisfied, and I resonate with C. S. Lewis, who wrote, "If I find in myself a desire which no experience in this world can satisfy, the most probable explanation is that I was made for another world."[9]

I am an earthbound creature living in a world where everything I know that has life seems to die. I do not believe this is how things were meant to be. It isn't the existence of death that I question, but the rightness of it. I have never known the death of another person to feel right. Of course, some deaths—those that bring an end to someone's suffering or pain—seem merciful. In those cases, death is sometimes even welcomed by both the living and the dying. But the only time death is welcomed in those situations is when it serves to release someone from suffering, which seems as misplaced as death itself.

I believe death is an intruder and that "the whole world is waiting, on tiptoe, with expectation, for the moment when that resurrection life and power sweeps through it, filling it with the glory of God as the waters cover the sea."[10] And I take this on faith.

Which is harder to believe: that God could bring a frozen bird back to life in the hands of a fifteen-year-old boy, or that Christ himself has risen and that he will also raise me?

———

The bird did not come back to life. It remained as I had found it—frozen solid. What struck me was the authenticity of my own prayer. I really believed in a divine being who could do what I was asking—raise the dead. When I prayed that prayer, something warmed in me. What had just spilled out of me flowed from something real within—faith. Somewhere along the way I had accepted that there was an author of life—all life. I believed he not only could hear my prayer, but that, in fact, he *did*. Of course he did. There in the snow I had no reservations about this whatsoever. This represented a change in me. I wasn't perfect, or wise, or even obedient to the commands of Scripture. Not even close. But the effortlessness of that prayer showed me that somehow, at some time, I had become a person of faith. I genuinely believed that life would prevail over death.

———

Now my faith is being tested in ways I never imagined. I am in the early stages of heart failure. My doctor tells me I need open-heart surgery if I am to survive. So right now, I am doing my best to pay attention to what is happening with me. I am standing out on the ledge I have trusted all these years since that winter day, and I am tapping it with my foot, feeling for the slightest tremble, wondering if in this particular winter my faith will hold.

Unlike my father weeping or Dusty dying, the mortality I now face is my own. The sight of my father silently shaking in his chair made me wonder what else I did not know about him. Now that I have been told that my life is in jeopardy, I wonder what I will come to discover about myself.

I will be in the hands of people who have given their academic and professional lives to becoming experts in matters that relate specifically to my survival. I wonder what will happen. I wonder if this season of treatments, surgery, rehab, and setbacks will expose that boy in the snow as a fool. Will my faith tuck its tail and run now that I have come face to face with my own mortality? Will I feel alone and abandoned by God? What will become of my faith now that I am more like the bird than the boy?

CHAPTER **3**

THE SACRAMENTAL ECHO

Diagnosis

*You formed my inward parts; you
knitted me together in my mother's womb.
I praise you, for I am fearfully and wonderfully made.
Wonderful are your works; my soul knows it very well.*

PSALM 139:13-14

I watched the ceiling tiles pass overhead as the radiology nurse wheeled my gurney into the lab where she would perform my echocardiogram. The dimly lit room smelled nice—like apples. The temperature was warmer than the hall outside; it was a pleasant warmth. Classical music played so quietly that if I shifted in the bed, the sound of the sheets would cancel it out. My nurse explained what was about to happen in the same kind voice I imagined she used to read bedtime stories to the children in the frame sitting on her desk. She draped a blanket over me, told me to get comfortable, and then left me there alone.

The room felt familiar, like I had been there before. This was my first echocardiogram, so I knew I had never been in this particular room. But I had been somewhere like it. More than once, too. But when?

Then I remembered. My babies.

My wife, Lisa, and I have four children. During the doctor visits leading up to each of their births, she and I were taken into rooms just like this one—peaceful, spacious, warm, and clean. We would take our places—she on the paper-covered bed and me in the chair beside her—both of us wide-eyed with nervous excitement waiting for the doctor to come in and show us something we could hardly believe was possible, images of our unborn children kicking away in utero.

The first time we went in for an ultrasound I was surprised that the equipment wasn't larger, given the task it was built to perform. The sonogram machine stationed next to the bed didn't look like much more than a low-profile computer cart with a few unfamiliar accessories stowed neatly in their places. Surely a wonder like the one we were about to behold required my wife to be squeezed into some sort of high-tech tube. Or if not that, shouldn't there at least be a luminous belly-shaped dome on a large mechanical arm controlled by a technician behind a wall of glass? This room had neither. There was just a computer, a display screen, a half-moon-shaped wand, and a squeeze bottle of warm lubricating gel.

During one of the sonograms late in the pregnancy with our first child, our doctor pressed the jelly-covered wand against my wife's side and we saw our baby's face for the first time—clear as a photo. We saw two eyes, a button nose, puckered lips, and wisps of hair swirling in the amniotic fluid. Next the doctor showed us tiny little legs and arms, knees and elbows, fingers and toes. Then, with a bit of flourish, she showed us the evidence of our baby's gender. This little stranger was a boy. A son. *My* son.

The weight of this discovery was a lot to take in. Big questions rose up in my mind. What would he need from me? He would need everything. What could I give him? Not nearly enough. But whatever this little boy needed, I would find a way to get it. I was going to have a son.

The doctor resumed her tour of our boy's still-forming body and stopped on something I can close my eyes and see even now. She showed us his heart. We all went quiet for a sacred moment and watched it fluttering away there behind his little ribs. The chambers pumped in such a precise rhythm; it looked like something set in motion by a master clock maker—one little heart in the womb beating just inches away from his mother's. *Lub dub, lub dub.* What a wonder.

I had no idea how my son's heart knew to beat. But it did. It looked so meticulous yet so fragile. If it stopped, who could start it again? For that matter, when did it start in the first place—that first little flutter? Long ago Jesus of Nazareth said, "[The sower] sleeps and rises night and day, and the seed sprouts and grows; he knows not how."[1] Seeing my little boy's chambers and valves keeping time to some mysterious cadence no ear has ever heard awakened anew in me a reverence for life and its Author.[2] That reverence remains.

⌁⌁⌁

I hear the door open behind me. Someone is in the room with me now. My nurse comes around to the foot of my bed so I can see her before she says hello. In her motherly way she asks for my name and birthday, as if we haven't met. These are the two questions every staff person is required to ask to make sure they have the right patient. The correct answers, of course, are written on her charts. They are also printed on my armband. We both have cheat sheets.

I think it is funny that these routine questions are two of the most existential questions one human being could ever put to another: "Who are you and when did you come into this world?" But she isn't asking for my hopes and dreams here. She just needs a name and a date.

I say, "Russ Ramsey, five, seventeen, seventy-three."

"Really? Well, that's coming right up, isn't it?" she says looking at her chart. "In case I don't see you then, happy birthday. What brings you here today?"

I had been running a fever for three weeks. For the first week or so I assumed it was a virus, but after the standard nine-day viral lifespan passed, the fever persisted. I went to a clinic and got a bottle of antibiotics, but they didn't help. So I made an appointment with my doctor who told me it would be a few days before he could see me. When my appointment arrived, my doctor listened to my story with a look of concern. He told me no one should have a fever for this long. When he checked my vital signs, he discovered that I had a heart murmur. He asked if I knew about it. I did. Doctors found it during a routine physical when I was in high school. Back then they weren't too concerned. I had a misshaped valve, but my heart seemed to be working fine. Overall, I was a healthy kid.

But that was twenty-two years ago. My doctor explained that mine was a rather pronounced murmur. His concern was that one of my heart valves might be providing a place for blood-borne bacteria to hide. The human body is designed to be an inhospitable place for pathogens, but when parts of our bodies deviate from normal development—as with, for example, a misshapen heart valve—bacteria can sometimes find a fold in the tissue to latch onto and multiply. Doctors call this a vegetation.

During that first visit, my doctor sent me over to the lab for bloodwork to see if this was what was going on with me. Those cultures came back positive. I had high levels of bacteria in my bloodstream. As soon as he saw the results, he called and told me he wanted me to go to the emergency room. I needed to be admitted to the hospital because an infection like this could only be treated with IV antibiotics.

That was what brought me to the hospital.

What brought me in for the echocardiogram, however, was not the fever but the heart murmur. In the process of going through all the tests and physician consults, my doctors—a team which had quickly grown to include representatives from internal medicine, intensive care, infectious disease, cardiology, and, to my surprise, cardiac surgery—shifted their focus from the bacteria and fever (which they were now successfully treating with IV antibiotics) to that murmur everyone wanted to hear.

My hospital was a teaching hospital. This meant I rarely saw just one doctor at a time. Usually four or five of them would come in together—physicians and med students standing in a semicircle at the foot of my bed. They would take turns listening to my heart—often two at a time—and almost all of them would say something like, "Wow. That's quite a murmur," as they stepped aside to let another sortie of stethoscopes come in for a landing.

If that bacteria had attached itself to my heart valve, it might have done some damage. They wanted to have a better look.

That was what brought me in for the echocardiogram.

―〰〰―

I am a pastor. I spend time tracing my way through the old, old story of God's redemption—from the foundations of the world to where I and the people I minister to live today. I pray. I study the Bible and try, by God's mercy and help, to communicate what it says in such a way that it hides itself in the hearts of my hearers. I counsel people. And I administer the sacraments—those outward physical signs of inward spiritual realities.

What happened there in that radiology lab was sacramental. The nurse covered the wand with the warm gel, like a priest preparing the elements. As soon as she touched that sensor against my side the sonogram screen, which up until that point had been blank, filled with indecipherable swirls and streaks of gray. Then, as if coming into a clearing, we saw what we had come to see—my heart beating in real time. I had never seen this before.

Neither of us said anything. She made some notes and took a few measurements, and I watched in rapt attention as it pulsed away with clocklike precision, just like my unborn son's. I could see the distinct chambers on the right side of my heart contract and relax. I watched the tricuspid valve open as my aortic and pulmonary valves shut. Then, as quickly as they shut they opened again as my tricuspid closed. This was what my heartbeat looked like. The valves worked in perfect union, each functioning in its intended role to draw oxygenated blood from my lungs and send it through to the rest of my body.

The radiology nurse stayed on the right side of my heart for a few minutes, making notes, before moving over to the left. That was when I saw what had brought me to her. I saw my mitral valve—the valve that lets oxygen-rich blood into my left ventricle, the heart's main pumping chamber. Once the left ventricle was full, the mitral valve was supposed to close to keep the blood from regurgitating back into the heart as the ventricle pushed it out into my body. That was what was supposed to happen.

When we saw my mitral valve, the nurse stopped taking notes and measurements, and the two of us watched it in silence. This valve looked nothing like the others we had just seen. The others looked like tiny little gates opening and closing to a metronome. But my mitral valve looked like two pieces of spaghetti flapping around with no apparent purpose or design. This wasn't right. The nurse knew it, and I knew it too.

I said, "That's my murmur, isn't it?"

"You know I'm not supposed to read this for you. That's for your doctor." The force of her response was a reaction to what we were seeing.

"I'm not asking you to read it for me. But you and I both know a murmur brought me here, and all I'm asking you is if that's it."

She relaxed, "Yes. That is your murmur."

As she went back to her measurements and notes, I said, "It's sacramental."

⁓⁓⁓

The physical reality on that screen told me two things: there was a problem with my heart, and there was nothing I could do to fix it. I thought about the spiritual parallels. If I left my heart alone, who could say what would come of me. But to fix it I needed help, someone who understood the heart, how mine worked, how it was meant to work, what specifically in mine was broken, and what of it could be restored.

I thought about how the Psalms say we are fearfully and wonderfully made.[3] Our bodies are filled with wonderful redundancies that keep us alive when other parts of us are failing. Sometime after the echo, the doctor who read it said I might as well not have a mitral valve for all the good mine was doing. He told me my other

chambers and valves were working four times harder than normal
to make up for it, and though they were under constant pressure,
stretching and squeezing to compensate, they were getting the job
done and probably had been for some time.

Still, we are fragile. My particular blood-borne bacteria had
latched on to that misshapen valve and seemed to have chewed it
up. My doctors had a growing concern about how long the other
parts of my heart could compensate before giving out themselves.
My doctor cautioned me about not being too active until they
could decide how to treat me. He said, "You are in the early stages
of heart failure, and you need to understand that the heart you have
now is not the same as the one you had before you got sick."

Half joking, so I could digest his words, I said, "So if this had
happened a hundred years ago . . ."

"You would be dead by the end of the year. No question," he said.

But this is not a hundred years ago. This is today, and today I live
a few miles away from one of the best hospitals in the world with
a team of physicians who have seen patients like me come through
their operating rooms many times. The heart work I need is something my doctor tells me he knows how to do, and he will do it.

This, like the sonogram room, felt familiar. It felt like my journey
into faith. That I with my failing heart could have fallen as I had
into the hands of someone who not only understood how to fix me
but then had the courage to open me up and do the work was a
fearful and wonderful sacramental thought.[4] And I remembered
that this had been done for me once before.

My own journey into the Christian faith carried with it the
echoes of being born into something new. At fifteen I made a
profession of faith in Jesus, and I cannot think of anything in my
life that hasn't been affected in one way or another by that decision.
Faith is a journey—"a long obedience in the same direction."[5] To

walk in faith is to confess that we do not know what awaits us, and the faith I have embraced does not promise an easy road.[6] Nevertheless, it is my road, and I will walk it. What else can I do?

Still, as I watch the failed remnants of my mitral valve flapping away on the sonogram screen, I cannot help but think that perhaps my life, up to this point, has taken place in a kind of womb from which I am about to be delivered.

CHAPTER **4**

TRAIL MAGIC

Hospitalization and Adaptation

*All adventures happen in that damned and magical
space, wherever it may be found or chanced
upon, which least resembles one's home.*

MICHAEL CHABON

To walk in faith is to confess that we do not know what awaits us. I am trying not to lose the trail.

A few summers ago I hiked across the state of Missouri. I followed the Katy Trail, an old railroad that was converted into a 250-mile greenway from east of Kansas City to St. Louis. Knowing there were little towns every five or ten miles, I didn't carry much—just some water, a few snacks, a notebook, a change of clothes, and a small emergency shelter.

There was one notorious eighteen-mile stretch of open fields along the Missouri River that offered nothing in the way of clean water or shelter. When I came to this section I had already covered twenty miles that day. Though it was getting late and I was tired, I decided to tackle those eighteen miles with the promise that I would give myself a nice meal once I got to the town on the other side.

With thirteen miles to go, I ran out of water. The summer sun ratcheted temperatures into the high nineties and there was no shade to be found. I was in trouble. To make it to safety I had to keep moving, but if I didn't rest I might fall prey to heatstroke. I needed water, but I would have to sweat out what little I retained in order to get more. Even though I knew where I was and that help was not far away, I suddenly felt lost.

These are critical moments for hikers. The greatest danger in a situation like this is not the hunger or thirst but the inability to think straight. When hikers lose the trail, if they aren't thinking rationally they will often make decisions that will lead them even farther away from safety.

I wanted to leave the trail and cut across the fields to see if I could find water, but I knew that was a dangerous idea. I staggered on, slowly but always in motion. I felt my energy wicking away.

Then I saw a bench up ahead—one of the Lewis and Clark historical markers that dotted the trail. I decided I would hike to the bench and reward myself with a short rest. Not too long. I had to keep moving. Time was against me.

As I approached the bench I saw something I had only read about in backpacking articles—trail magic. There under the bench in its shade sat a small bottle of water and an energy bar. Trail angels had been here. Trail angels are people who leave little caches of supplies along difficult stretches of the trail to help wanderers who realize too late that they are not equipped to finish what they so confidently began—wanderers like me.

Right now, in this fragile state, I feel like I could use a little trail magic. With every passing day I am beginning to fear that it would be easy for me to wander down into the willowy thickets of the heart and lose the trail, but I don't know if that is happening. We seldom know when we are in the process of getting lost. I need to keep my head on straight.

This trail started with a fever. The fever led to the doctor's office. The doctor's office led to a blood test. The blood test led to a phone call. I answered thinking it was my doctor calling to give me the results. I remember taking his call. I was at my office. It was around 11:00 a.m. I stepped out into the parking lot because of the poor reception in the building.

I listened as he told me that I needed to be hospitalized immediately. He had already called the emergency room. They were expecting me. I don't remember driving myself to the hospital, but I remember calling my wife. I told her what was happening and asked her not to bring the kids until I was settled in a room. I didn't want them to see me until we knew what we were dealing with. I wanted to make sure I was thinking clearly.

I spoke with my children on the phone after they got out of school. I assured them I was okay. The younger ones, the ones under ten, didn't seem to understand the situation—just that I was sick and wouldn't be home that night. The older ones carried it differently. I could hear it in their voices; this was unfamiliar terrain.

That first day in the hospital was chaotic. I changed rooms a few times. The second day was full of testing and radiology. The third day, Thursday, I finally got settled in. I spent most of that day waiting for my test results to come back so the infectious disease doctors could determine how to treat me. I called my wife and asked her to bring the kids.

After I hung up, a cardiac surgeon—a man I had not yet met but who would soon hold my heart in his hands—dropped by to tell me they had seen an issue on my echocardiogram and that I was in the early stages of heart failure and would need open-heart surgery.

This was the first time those words were spoken to me.

"When?" I asked.

"In a perfect world, we would do it tomorrow. But we have to wait until we've dealt with your infection. So probably in a few weeks."

With all due respect to my surgeon, in a perfect world he would be out of a job. But that is not our world. Just as he finished explaining what needed to be done, my children burst into the room, smiling and bearing little gifts. At the sight of them I felt the breath go out of my lungs, and I began to weep. The news of the severity of my situation collided with the sight of these precious children I had not seen since I dropped them off at school a few days earlier. My children stood frozen in the doorway, unsure of what to do at the sight of their father shaking with grief.

I hurt. My soul ached for a different world. Each of my children suddenly had tears in their eyes. My affliction had, in some measure, just become their burden. I watched it happen right in front of me. They had never seen me shaking like this before. I imagine the image is burned into their memories in the same way the sight of my father weeping in his chair remains burned into mine.

No one was trying to hurt us. No one had done anything wrong. But the world we inhabit is one where children feel sorrow long before they have the words to express it. It just hits them like a punch to the gut and hollows out a part of their insides. They do not understand it, but they feel it and remember it.

I asked the surgeon to take my wife into the hall and tell her what he had just told me. I snuggled my two youngest daughters in next to me, one on either side. I told them that I missed them.

They told me they missed me too. They presented me with some cards they had made, dabbed at my tears with a tissue, and ate my pudding. Then Lisa came in, processing what the surgeon had told her.

She looked strong, resolved to face whatever was headed our way. This was not my burden to carry alone. It was hers too. She has been this way for as long as I have known her.

After Lisa took the kids home, she came back. She wanted to be with me at midnight so she could tell me happy birthday. The love I felt for her that night was unexpected. I have loved her for as long as I have known her, and we have had a happy marriage. The love itself wasn't new; the way I felt it was. She and I had been married for close to eighteen years. We made a promise to each other all those years ago that we would love one another in sickness and in health, come what may, until death separated us. Still, neither of us had ever come this close to having to keep that particular vow.

But there she was, unwaveringly present in my sorrow, in my pain, in my fear, and in my waiting. We talked about what lay ahead. Then shortly after midnight she kissed me and went home.

For my birthday, Lisa and I had planned to throw a large party at the house, invite all our friends, spend more money than we could afford, and sit by the fire late into the evening laughing, sipping drinks, and telling stories. That was the plan.

Early on, my medical team held out hope that I might be released in time for Friday's party. But the infection proved difficult to identify and, as a consequence, difficult to treat. So on Thursday afternoon, my doctor told me I would be staying for the weekend.

Birthdays invite a certain kind of lonesomeness and intro-spection. We ask, *Am I still young? Is my life what I hoped it would be? Am I happy?*

While I normally deal well with birthdays, I wrestled with a sober, if arbitrary, pensiveness about turning forty. To my wife, I called it the "halfway-point syndrome." My struggle only inten-sified when my cardiac surgeon announced the change of venue for my party by telling me that I was dying.

A few friends came to visit. One brought me a bottle of twelve-year-old scotch. My children made more cards and gave me some of their favorite stuffed animals, which I kept in the bed with me until my doctors sent me home. The scotch stayed in the bottle.

My shift nurse also brought me a gift—an eviction notice. The lab had identified my infection as a strep, and they were in the process of setting me up with a regimen of IV antibiotics that I could administer from home. In the morning, they would send me down to radiology for a PICC line—a plastic catheter they would insert into the basilic vein in my right arm and feed almost all the way up into my heart. The PICC line would deliver the antibiotics directly to the source of the infection. Once insurance signed off on my medicine and the PICC line was in, I would be cleared to go home.

Around the dinner hour visitors stopped coming. Lisa took the kids back to the house, and I found myself alone flipping through the channels as I waited for my Salisbury steak and vegetable medley.

It was a good birthday, I told myself. *It's okay. You are going to be okay.* I was trying not to lose the trail.

There was a knock on my door. An older African American woman poked her head in and said, "I have your dinner."

She walked over to my bed, set the tray down on the table beside me, looked at the number on my ID bracelet, and asked me for my name and date of birth.

"Russell Brown Ramsey, five, seventeen, seventy-three."

She nodded, started to leave, and then stopped.

"Wait," she said. "Today is your birthday?"

"It is."

She straightened herself up, turned to face me, and put her right hand over her left—a portrait of dignity and poise. And then, with just the two of us in the room, she began to sing over me:

Happy birthday to you.
Happy birthday to you.
Happy birthday, dear Mr. Ramsey.
Happy birthday to you.

Then she smiled at me, turned, and left the room.

I wept. Trail magic.

Often the best gifts we can give each other cost nothing.

This woman did not know me, but she knew this stretch of trail. She didn't know if I was kind or mean, gentle or abrasive, honest or a liar. She didn't need to know what I had accomplished in life or what I had wasted. She just knew that if I was there in her hospital on my birthday, I was probably feeling a little lost. On that basis alone, I mattered to her.

Questions about whether my life had measured up to my own expectations as I reached the halfway point seemed to disappear when this woman I did not know took a moment out of her day

to express, in such a simple yet intimate way, that she was happy
I was born.

In that moment I genuinely was too.

She fed me with kindness. I felt its power. I feel it still.

CHAPTER 5

THE DISTANCE

The Space Between the
Sick and the Well

Do you who live in radiance hear the prayers of those
of us who live in skin? We have a love that's not as
patient as yours was. Still, we do love now and then.

RICH MULLINS

I did not anticipate this distance I feel. Distance from others. From God.

I am at home now, tethered to a fanny pack that holds a machine that pumps IV antibiotics directly into my heart through a catheter in my arm. There is a drawer in my refrigerator full of very expensive medicine. On my dining table sits a red tray with a large box of sterile latex gloves, alcohol swabs, and syringes of saline solution used to flush the PICC line when I change my medications.

The pump runs twenty-four hours a day. I can feel the medicine in my blood. I run the numbers. In the two weeks since I was first admitted to the hospital, I have had over six gallons of antibiotics pumped into my system. I feel syrupy and sluggish.

Once the IV treatments have killed all the bacteria and my blood tests come back clean, we will schedule open-heart surgery. My surgeon wants to do this as soon as possible. Who am I to argue?

I cannot remember what it feels like to be well. This is not as much of a complaint as an observation. Like a frog in a pot, over time I've grown accustomed to the effects of my infection—the night sweats, the constant chill, my foggy mind, the ache when I stand up, my general malaise.

I have a recurring dream that wakes me with a start. I can never retain the details, only that in it I was afraid. In the dream I am being chased, but that is all I can recall. I wake trembling with fear. It takes a few minutes to remember where I am and shake it off. When I lay back down, my pillow is drenched in cold sweat. I go through this routine alone almost every night. I do not wake my wife, and I don't think to talk about it during the day. But every night when everyone else in the house is sound asleep, I am frightened awake. And I am the only one who knows it. Whether it be the hound of heaven or the devils of hell, this is my nightmare. It has become part of the rhythm of my day. It happens so often now that it feels normal.

The fever has given me an ashen complexion. My friends tell me I look gray. They are deeply concerned when they say it. I see it in their eyes and in the ways they choose their words. They want to say the right thing but don't know what that is, so sometimes they say the wrong thing. I understand. I say the wrong things too. Sometimes I make little jokes about dying.

There is a strange relational order to this experience. I feel a great burden to care for loved ones who, themselves, are afraid for me. I don't know what hounds are chasing them in secret, but I see their fear when they ask me to tell them my story. So I try to tell it in a way that will comfort them. I want to reassure them that I will be fine. But I do not know if that is true.

Nevertheless I, the infirm, find myself caring for the sorrows and fears of the well. I do not resent them for this, not even a little. I love my friends. I want to comfort them. I am a pastor. Caring for the hearts of others is part of my profession. But walking through suffering is a work that is bound by limitation. Often it isn't that the afflicted are unwilling to let others in. It is just that there comes a certain point in a person's suffering where there is no apparent port of entry.

I experienced this inaccessibility when a friend of mine who lost a child wrote to me in the rawness of his grief. He told me how he held the body of his little boy in his arms and cried out to God for the miracle of life. He covered his son's face with his tears and breathed the boy's hair into his mouth with every sob. He wrote, "I wanted to consume him, and swallow death, and see him live."

This walk through suffering follows a lonesome road. I wanted to do for my friend's sorrow what he wanted to do for his son's death; I wanted to consume it. But that was not mine to do. I could venture only so far into his pain before I could go no further. Those words he sent were his way of coming out to meet me. Still, it was like we were speaking over a fence.

My suffering is not so severe, though I do sense a distance between myself and those I love. To close the gap, I have to come out of my present distress to meet them just as they have to step into a suffering that is not their own to meet me. If I wanted, I suppose I could withdraw from people on the basis that they don't understand my pain. And in a sense I would be right. But what sort of fool would require such a thing of those who only want to love me?

My affliction has provided something people rarely possess—objective data that my heart is failing. But in truth, my position is really no different from anyone else's—not when it comes to the question of our mortality. The only real difference between us is that certain pieces of information about my current position in this world are known. But no one is promised tomorrow. Some of the very people who are afraid of losing me might well be taken from this world long before I go. Who is to say?

Still, the raw, clinical data about the severity of my condition leads to a sense of distance. It is the feeling that I am in one place and everyone else is in another. It is a distance born out of love and concern. And fear. But it remains a distance—one I suspect has been here all along but has now stepped into a light by which it may be seen. The fear of losing me has illuminated the truth that no one has any power to keep me. Though there are hounds in the shadows bearing down on us all, we have caught a glimpse of mine.

I wish I could take away their fear. Here is that strange relational order again. I see people trying to imagine being in my position. They say this must be very difficult for me. Then I do the same with them. I imagine how sad they must feel worrying about someone they love. That must be difficult for them.

In truth, I do know what they're feeling. I feel it whenever I think about my friend Barbara. Barbara is just a few years older than me. Her family and mine have been in a fellowship group together for four years. Our lives are intertwined.

Barbara is one of the living ones—a saint with a blue streak. She has that rare ability to get things done quickly while making those around her feel like she has all the time in the world for them. She is a woman who has many friends who all count her as their best friend, and none of them are mistaken. She is full of grace and moxie; the Lord is with her.

Barbara is battling cancer. She has been in this fight for over five years. She lives her life snapping back and forth between progress and setbacks. Her husband, children, and friends snap with her. I am one of those friends. We struggle with her disease, though she works hard to lead us well. But because we are not her, no matter how close we would like to be, we have no choice but to watch her suffering from at least somewhat of a distance.

It is hard for her to go through. It is hard for us to watch.

Like Barbara, I have now become a prayer request.

More people than I can count have told me they are praying for my family and me. I am touched by the idea that we are so greatly loved from such a distance. When people who have been praying for me come to see me, they hope for news that their prayers are being answered. So I try to measure my words to encourage their faith.

"I'm better than I was," I say. "My doctors assure me I'll be fine."

I try to be my normal self. But there is a PICC line in my arm and a fanny pack around my waist with a machine that makes a little ticking noise as it pumps its syrup into my heart. So there is a distance between us.

I tire easily. I don't have much strength. I find myself sitting down while everyone else is standing. They now must look down on me.

"I'm better than I was."

Prayer is more complicated than it used to be. It isn't that I have trouble praying or doubt that God hears me. It's that I don't know what God has in mind for me. When I pray, as Jesus taught his disciples, "Not my will, but yours, be done,"[1] I feel that the stakes are somehow suddenly higher, even though I know on an intellectual level that it is an error to think that the stakes have ever been lower.

My prayers now feel more like an exercise in surrender than a conversation. For most of my life I have prayed to a God I believe made and sustains the universe. I have always believed him to be good. But now my faith requires me to entertain the question of whether I can say with Job, "Though he slay me, I will hope in him."[2]

I think I can, if he helps me. But I am aware in new ways that the God I believe in is not one to keep us from affliction. Rather, he is one who works through it. His ways are not my ways, and his thoughts are not my thoughts.[3] If I take the position that something must make sense to me if I am to believe it makes any sense at all, can I still call myself a man of faith—one who believes in what cannot be known and hopes in what is unseen?[4] What sort of faith could I honestly claim if I required the God I believed in to only do what made sense to this earthbound creature?

Here again is distance. His ways are not my ways, and his thoughts are not my thoughts.

These days my prayers are filled with things I do not understand, and they are spoken to a God I do not understand. Surely the same must be true of those who are praying for me.

~~~~~~

I realize I have a choice about how I regard this distance. I have a choice in how I respond to people when they say the wrong thing or avoid me because they don't know what to say. The lines have fallen in strange places for us all. Who knows what the rules of engagement are? I don't want to become so self-important that I require a certain kind of elegance from those who stumble around this unfamiliar stage.

It serves no purpose for me to be touchy about how people interact with me or I with them. We live most of our days avoiding the subject of our mortality. It takes courage to face death, and trying to be brave is the same as being brave.

The truth is, I don't always know how to be. If I encourage people to take a casual approach toward my affliction, am I robbing them of the opportunity to express what they really feel? If I treat my situation with utmost solemnity, am I being unnecessarily morbid?

I talked with Barbara about this. She told me that when her hair started to fall out after her first round of chemotherapy, she and her daughters went into their backyard and she shook and rubbed her head until there were no loose hairs left. She said it looked like a ginger snow as her red hair just kept falling and falling. They cried at first, until they burst into laughter.

It was both tragic and comic. All comedy is. And so is all affliction.

In affliction we cry and then we laugh. Or we laugh and then we cry. We become schooled in the art of being able to feel more than one thing at a time—a sure indicator of spiritual maturity. Since the afflicted live among the well, moments like these are bound to come. And with them, this feeling of distance.

But it does not need to be a separating distance. Just as I must not demand that I understand everything God is doing in order to pray to him, I cannot expect others to understand everything I am experiencing in order for them to talk to me. The distance is real. The least I can do is come out to meet those who seek me. Like a docent in a museum, I can try to explain what they are seeing. I can try to help.

I am the steward of this sacred distance. Since it is something I cannot erase, I shall become its curator instead.

CHAPTER 6

THE LETTERS

Putting a House in Order

Be filled with envy and anger for those
who are still healthy. Wail, plead, beg,
make deals with friends and with the Infinite.
Sink into despair. Lie down in hopelessness.
Die then—even before you die. Or else, prepare.
Long before that final confrontation, prepare.

WALT WANGERIN JR.

In less than twenty-four hours I will be lying unconscious on an operating table. My wrists and ankles will be in restraints, and I will have a breathing tube down my throat. My chest will be open, and a machine on a cart beside me will perform the work of my heart and lungs while a surgeon and his team attempt to repair—or if that's not possible, replace—my mitral valve.

Mitral valve repair is a relatively safe surgery, my surgeon tells me. Routine, even. I am confident everything will go according to plan and I will emerge from the anesthesia sore but ready and eager to rehabilitate. Still, I have agreed to let a team of doctors stop my heart tomorrow in order to remove a part of it and then sew it back up and start it again. Because of this, I have been making certain preparations.

Ten years ago as a young pastor, I met a woman named Alice. She was in the late stages of a very aggressive cancer. She had recently moved to my city so she could spend the last weeks of her life close to her daughters. One Sunday Alice and her girls visited our church. She wore a floral-print bandana on her head because the chemotherapy had taken her hair. I introduced myself after the service, and she asked if I could meet with her for a cup of coffee.

We met the next day, and Alice told me some of her story. She had experienced more pain, loss, and grief in her fifty-one years than anyone I could recall, and that was all before she found out she had terminal cancer. Somewhere in all her Job-like suffering she had become a believer in Jesus Christ who, she told me with the joyful sincerity of a child, had promised not to let her go.

I asked what brought her to our church.

"I want you to bury me."

With those six words, Alice defined who we would be to one another.

The apostle Paul, in his first letter to the church in Corinth, argues that what other people think about us doesn't matter.[1] He goes on to say that what we think about ourselves doesn't really matter either. All that matters is what God thinks about us, because he is the only one who sees us as we truly are.

One of the sad burdens many of us carry in this life comes to us when we accept the lie that our worth is determined by what other people think. This is an incredible power we hand over to others, many of whom never even know we have given it to them. Whether it is the young man trying to win the affection of the pretty girl, or the middle-aged man sinking into depression because he believes he has failed to accomplish anything anyone would ever regard as a legacy, or any one of us choosing our spending habits, clothing, or words in order to be accepted into someone else's community—we all want to belong, and we go to great lengths to establish our worthiness. We often lose ourselves in this process.

Conversely, one of the great joys in this life is found in those rare relationships where neither person is trying to prove anything to the other because they know, with confidence and a clear conscience, who they are to one another before God.

It would be so freeing if we could sweep our arm across the surface of our complicated relationships, clearing away everything until all that remained was just the two of us as we really were—no distractions, no props, no clutter. Few things sweep away the clutter of our fears like coming face to face with our own mortality. When this happens, life gets simple in a hurry.

⁓

"I want you to bury me."

In our first meeting, those six words swept across the table between Alice and me. We knew who we were to each other from the start. She was a woman about to die, and I was the minister who would hold her hand and speak words of truth until she did, after which I would commend her body to the earth and her soul to the Lord she loved and trusted so deeply. And I would comfort her family along the way.

I told Alice that I had never performed a funeral. She told me not to worry. She had given hers a lot of thought, and we could plan it together. And that we did, down to the songs, the Scripture readings, and the balloons we released at her gravesite. I have always counted it as a gift from God that my friend Alice, the woman in the casket, helped me compose the first funeral I officiated as a young pastor.

One of the things Alice asked me to help her do during the last week of her life was compose letters to her children, which I would give to them at her graveside.

What goes into a letter from a dying mother to her weary, angry, grieving adult children? Intimate things I will not spell out in detail, except to say that along with those intimate things, she also wanted to talk about ultimate things. She wanted to write about what she hoped would come of them. She wanted to articulate those prayers that rose to her lips when she thought about her girls moving into their midtwenties without her.

"I want them to know Jesus," she said. "Tell them I know this hurts. I know life has been hard. I know they are confused and angry with God. But tell them my deepest desire is that my children would walk with Jesus and know the comfort of his love, just as I have."

Alice knew she wasn't long for this world. As far as I know, I have no reason to think such things about my present situation. I am told a lot would have to go wrong for me to be in any sort of mortal danger. But still, as King Solomon wrote, "no one can discover anything about their future."[2] What I do know is that for several hours tomorrow, my heart will be stopped. So in light of that reality, I have been putting my house in order.

One of my coworkers is a notary public. Yesterday my wife and I went to see her in order to draw up a durable power-of-attorney document in which I gave my wife full authority to both approve and reject life-sustaining measures if necessary.

The document states: "If I should ever reach the point at which my doctor believes I am going to die no matter what is done, I direct this person to ensure that I am allowed to die naturally. That means not starting or continuing to use machines or treatments that would only prolong my dying. At that point, this person should ensure that I have only the medicine or treatment that I need to keep me comfortable and relieve pain."

I called in two other coworkers who watched as we signed. Then they signed the document as well, affirming that they had witnessed the transaction. We hugged them and thanked them, aware of the distance we all felt. After that, I wrote letters to my wife and children in case they needed them—letters about intimate and ultimate things.

What Alice wanted for her children is essentially what I want for mine. I want them to wrestle with Job's question—Shall we receive good from God and not receive sorrow too?[3] I want them to receive my letters as words of comfort and not bitterness. In this life, they will know good times, but they will also certainly know grief. This life is filled with sadness. When sorrow comes I pray they will have the humility to remember that God is still with them, though they see through a glass darkly.[4]

I pray they would see that all of history points to a gracious, loving God whose ways are higher than ours, but are nonetheless filled with unmatched mercy and grace.[5] I pray that when calamity befalls them, they would not stand shaking their fists at the heavens demanding that God give an account of himself.[6]

I pray they would trust him to be their Man of Sorrows, the one who has borne their grief and carried their sadness.[7]

I want them to need Christ more than they need anything or anyone else in this world—even their father. I want them to know that the cross and the resurrection of Jesus Christ are God's inscrutable manifesto concerning the depth of his love for them.[8] I want that to be the truth in which they live and move and have their being.[9] And I want the same for myself.

This is such a strange sort of gathering work I'm doing—gathering people and words to arrange for a future I cannot control. I cannot do this on my own. I need my friends. Soon after this all started, I called on my friend Andy. Andy is a musician. When he asked if there was anything he could do for me, I asked if he would help me record a song for my wife.

When my wife and I first met, I was a musician. I wrote a song about wanting to build a life with her. Now almost twenty years in, I have rewritten the song to reflect on the joy of having spent half our lives together.

As Andy and I worked on the track, we both understood that there were certain components that needed to be completed before my surgery—specifically, the lyrics and the vocals. He could finish the rest later. But those two components, like the letters, needed to be done before I went under. Though we never spoke the reasons why it needed to be this way, we both knew.

During our last day in the studio together, I asked if he would hold on to the letters I had written to my wife and kids. I told him I would come get them from him once I had recovered.

Tearfully, he took them from me. He put them on a shelf and said, "They'll be right here until you come for them."

"And you can finish the song, right? You have what you need?"

"Everything you need is right here," he assured me.

I was asking Andy to serve as a kind of a priest—to stand as my intermediary between the temporal and the eternal.

I know Andy loves me. He has for many years. I am thankful to have a friend I can call on to serve as my mediator should I require one. I know he feels the sacred significance of his involvement in this as well. His priestly duties here will mark our friendship for as long as we share it.

When I think about Andy with those letters, I remember that much of the nature of friendship is priestly; it is the work of carrying one another. I gave Andy five sealed letters in case the worst arrived. But he and I have carried other burdens just as great as those. We have borne each other's struggles, fears, sins, and secrets. He was an obvious choice to hold my words.

My wife does not know what I have asked Andy to do. I pray I will get to be the one to tell her. I am confident I will. Nevertheless, I am in a place in my life where I have to consider my mortality.

I can be an impatient man. I can get lost in my work, my ambition, and my agenda. But these are the days where my Maker has used a blood-borne bacteria and a damaged mitral valve to sweep away the clutter and silence the noise, even if only for a while, so that I might put pen to paper to express my ultimate prayers and intimate hopes for the lives of these people I love.

So for this failing heart valve I bless the name of the Lord, come what may.[10]

And I prepare.

CHAPTER 7

SCOWLING AT THE ANGEL

Surgery and Waking Up

*The fruit of the Spirit is love, joy, peace, patience,
kindness, goodness, faithfulness, gentleness,
self-control; against such things there is no law.*

GALATIANS 5:22-23

We sat together in the lobby, just the two of us. The sun would be coming up any minute. We didn't say much. We couldn't. We were on the verge of bursting into tears, but neither of us did. What we did say was mostly of a light-hearted nature.

It was our eighteenth anniversary.

"In sickness and health," I joked.

"Yeah, well," she said, "it's only fair. You stuck with me through four labors and deliveries. It's the least I can do."

A man wearing black scrubs and carrying a clipboard entered the waiting area and barked, "Ramsey. *Ramsey.*"

Together we stood and made our way to the shouting man, who led us to the elevator.

"I'll be right out here," Lisa said. "I'll see you just as soon as they're done."

I squeezed her hand, gave her a kiss, handed her my wedding ring, and then stepped into the elevator as it closed and carried me up and away.

The man in black said, "If you have any modesty issues, now is the time to get over them." He spoke as though I had done something wrong and was about get my comeuppance. I do not know why he did this. He continued, "I'm taking you to the pre-op ward. The first thing they're going to have you do is strip down to nothing."

What he lacked in bedside manner he made up for in accuracy. A nurse met us at the door and led me to a room filled with beds separated only by curtains. He gave me a hand towel and told me to strip down so he could shave me.

"Um, what?" I asked.

"I need to shave you from your neck to your toes. Standard procedure for open-heart surgery," he said. "I'll be right here on the other side of the curtain. Go ahead and lie down on the bed when you're done. You can cover yourself with that towel. Holler at me when you're ready."

With no option but to comply, I played my only card: "You're going to bring me a sedative soon, right?"

He said, "Just as soon as I'm finished your surgical team will pay you a visit and set you up with an IV. They'll give you something then to help you relax."

I did as instructed. After he at last clicked off the electric shaver, my nurse draped a white cotton blanket over me, and then a second one, tucking them in tightly under my legs and sides, as if to say, "Sorry, friend. Here's a little of that modesty back."

I hadn't been that vulnerable since the day I was born.

As I waited I thought about Lisa down in the lobby. Never in eighteen years of marriage would we have imagined I would be lying in this bed, not at my age anyway. I thought about how strong she had been in the weeks leading up to this day, and how she had carried so much with such grace. Though we had kept the mood light in the waiting room, I knew, in a way only a husband of two decades could, a bit of the sorrow she now sat with. And I loved her for it.

The Puritans used to say you got married in order to fall in love. They reasoned: How can a man and woman possibly hope to know the wonder, joy, and depth of real love—the kind where you are truly known and truly loved at the same time—without making those two lives into one thing?

The qualities I love most about my wife were largely unknown to me when we married. We had known each other for a few years, but we both brought oceans of deep, unexplored waters to that altar. We promised to stay together in plenty and in want, in sickness and in health, for better or for worse, but neither of us knew what those words would cost or where they would take us. How could we? We were kids. Yet there we stood, she in her shimmering ivory and me in my rented tux—the angel and the penguin—promising, like a couple of immortals, to sound those depths together until one of us died.

But I could not have known how she would pour her love into our children, how she would build them up and guard their hearts. When we moved them away from their friends in one city to a place they didn't know, I watched this woman join them in a sorrow they were too young to name. I watched her grieve their heartache and risk new relationships to help them begin again.

I could not have known how she would lay down her life to support God's call on mine, or how she would count that as God's will for her as well without complaint, resentment, or doubt.

I could not know how she would fight for me to return to her when I would withdraw into myself out of fear, or how she would comfort me with gracious words when I felt lost and alone, or how she would confront me with a loving rebuke when I needed someone to break anxiety's spell.

I could not have known the home she would make for us— practical, happy, and beautiful. Or how she would remember her friends' joys and sorrows throughout the years—always ready to celebrate with real gladness or to mourn with genuine, tearful grief.

Now here we were, eighteen years later. With four cities, four kids, and probably four dozen W-2s between us, I marveled at the woman in the lobby making good yet again on her promise to stay. The penguin had no idea.

***

Soon my surgical team began their rounds. No fewer than a dozen people passed through my curtain, each armed with a medical device or a clipboard full of forms. After they had asked every question they needed to hear me answer—Did I know where I was? Did I know why I was there? Did I know my name and birthday?—they injected a warm liquid into my IV which left me awake but set me free from all of life's carking cares.

And so I went off to surgery in much the same way that I came into this world—completely vulnerable and swaddled in warm hospital cotton, watching the tiles pass overhead as they delivered me from my familiar warmth into the cold air and bright lights of the operating room. The last thought to pass through my mind before they took me completely under was that I would either wake up in recovery or in glory.

I first opened my eyes to a blurry figure in white standing at the foot of my bed, shining so bright I had to squint. Was this the angel dressed in lightning who sat atop Jesus' empty tomb on that first Easter morning, coming to tell me I had risen to newness of life?[1] Or had Abraham's visitor by the oaks of Mamre appeared to tell me to hang on just a little longer?[2] As I adjusted to the light I realized the vision in white was my wife in the sweater she put on that morning. She was the most beautiful thing I had ever seen— my friend, my heart, my love. Her glory flooded into the fog of my waking and I came to.

I heard the voices of doctors and nurses reading my vitals from the monitor above my head. I heard someone ask if I knew where I was. Though I don't remember many of the specifics, I remember that the tone in the room was relaxed and positive.

As I became more alert, my doctor performed a series of tests to gauge my overall condition. I squeezed his hand. I followed his penlight with my eyes. He asked me how I felt.

"I can't feel my left foot," I told him.

He asked, "What do you mean? Like it's asleep?"

I said, "No. I can't feel it at all."

He asked me to wiggle my toes. I couldn't. Not even a little. It wasn't just numb. My left foot was hanging limp off to the side like it didn't even belong to my body.

Not only was I unable to walk, I was unable to stand up on my own. Since my sternum was now a broken bone held together by titanium wires, I wasn't able to use my upper body to push up out of a chair, which is how most of us perform that task without a second thought. I needed my legs to do all the work, and I didn't have them.

Later my doctor told me that during surgery I experienced a "neurological event." Since he wasn't sure exactly what had happened, he didn't want to use the word "stroke."

He explained that blood wants to clot when it comes into contact with anything outside the body. Since my surgery required that I be hooked up to a heart-and-lung machine, my doctors put me on a blood thinner before starting the procedure in order to keep my blood from clotting when it passed through the pump's plastic tubing. Usually the blood thinners do their job, but the body's design to protect and heal itself means that sometimes even a blood thinner can't stop a tiny clot or two from forming when human blood comes into contact with a manmade material. Most likely this is what happened: a tiny clot formed when it hit that tubing and then traveled up into my brain where it got stuck and shut a few things down.

This was a problem because my nurses were determined to get me up on my feet as soon as possible. But without my left foot, I couldn't stand. This detail was irrelevant to my caretakers. They hoisted me and my lifeless leg to the standing position and forced me to walk by pushing and pulling one leg in front of the other. Eight feet from the bed to the window and eight feet back.

Every step was an exercise in defeat. I couldn't do it. I sulked. When I was young I used to walk wherever I wanted. But now I stretched out my hands and others carried me where I did not want to go.[3] I tried to object, but the neurological event had also shut down a significant part of my ability to speak so that I couldn't express my frustration. As they carried me across the room and back, my wife stayed where I could see her, encouraging me. She said she was proud of me.

When she told me she believed I could do this and that she loved me, I lifted my eyes to the vision in white—the wife of my youth—and focused all my confusion, pleading, anger, and frustration into a single venomous glare that said to her, "You leave me the hell alone."

Anesthesia is a strange monster. Anyone who has been through something even as simple as having their wisdom teeth removed has likely provided at least a few minutes of entertainment for their loved ones. It is one of those rare times when a man gets a free pass for whatever comes out of his mouth. But it is also true that traumatic situations do not create a person's character so much as they expose what is already there. Silence a man's inner dialogue and take away the filter through which he runs what he chooses to say and what he keeps inside, and what comes out of him will likely fall closer to the truth than to fiction. If this is true, then it is in me to belittle kindness and glare at beauty. It is in me to tell the ones who love me most to go away. It is in me to reject the advances of grace.

And it is true. I know it is.

I remember the first time I saw my wife. We were freshmen in college, less than a month in. I was sitting in the lounge outside the library when she passed through. My initial reaction was one of disbelief. She was the most beautiful girl I had seen in my short but attentive life. I had to do a double-take just to confirm that my eyes weren't playing a trick on me. Could someone really be that pretty? I resolved to find ways to put myself in her path in the hope that our roads might eventually converge into one.

Over the next four years we danced a dance that ultimately led us to this hospital room. She remained so radiant that when I woke from surgery I mistook her for an angel, or at the very least someone who had been draped in the splendor Moses brought down from the mountain to a fearful people.[4] But as it went with Moses and the children of Israel, my eyes grew accustomed to her glory, and I quickly moved from wonder to a familiarity that bred in me a heavily medicated yet nevertheless contemptible scowl. She took it without a word, dissolving my wrath with the soft answer of a smile.[5] She pulled her chair up next to my bed and lay her head down by my side.

─────

After I had been home for a couple of weeks, I asked her if she ever noticed that I gave her a few dirty looks. I remembered doing this but never knew if she had noticed. She told me I glared at her many times those first few days.

"Did it ever bother you?" I asked.

She told me she knew they came out of frustration. I was hurting and medicated, exposed and weak. I couldn't take myself to the bathroom or pour a drink of water. Often I couldn't even find the words to ask for help. Like a baby on his back, I made my needs known through tears and protest.

"Still, I'm sorry," I said. "What did you do when I scowled at you?"

"I cried," she said. "But never so you could see. I would step out into the hall or into the bathroom, cry my tears, and pull myself together before coming back."

"I made you leave?"

"No. Most of the time I would wait for you to fall asleep and then I would scoot my chair up next to the bed so that I could lay my head by your side and cry there."

I had no idea that was what she was doing when she lay her head by my side. All I remembered was that she was the picture of grace—steady and ever present, deflecting my misdirected frustration with a gentleness that won my heart. Hers was the voice of wisdom; all she spoke were words of kindness.[6] She lavished me with goodness and mercy. She filled the room with love, joy, and peace. She put my ring back on my finger, just as she had done eighteen years before, to say to me, "I still choose you." Against such things there is no law.[7]

There in my brokenness I had so little to give. But grace, she never left. She met me in all my frailty—raw and wrathful, as exposed and defenseless as the day I was born. There she stayed, tending to me with kindness and mercy, weeping both for her sorrow and mine while I slept, often in a chair scooted up next to my bed so that she could lay her head by my side because she loved me.

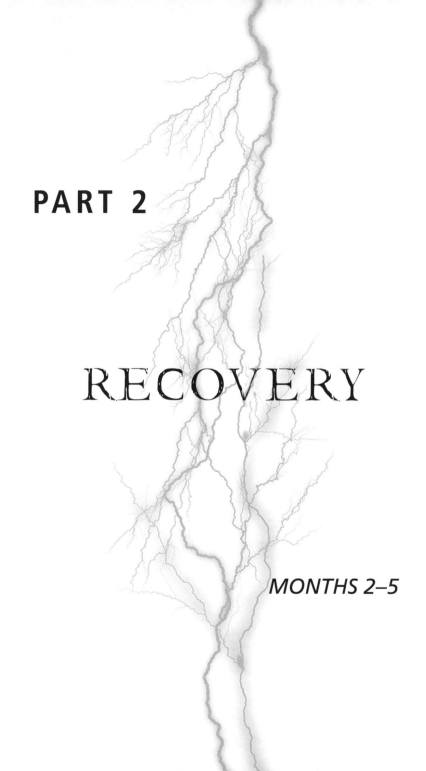

PART 2

RECOVERY

MONTHS 2–5

CHAPTER 8

SCAR TISSUE

Physical Healing and Resiliency

*Scars have the strange power to
remind us that our past is real.*

CORMAC McCARTHY

I bear on my body the marks of my affliction. By my count,
I have six new scars on the outside of my body, and four on the inside.

My four internal wounds consist of a broken sternum, an incision in the outer wall of my heart, another making a passage from
there into my left atrium, and another on my mitral valve itself.
There may be others, but those are the four I know.

My six external scars include a half-inch hole in the center of
my abdomen where a drainage tube used to be, a small incision on
the right side of my chest through which electrodes were inserted
into the wall of my heart in case it needed to be shocked back into
rhythm, a five-inch zipper scar down the center of my sternum, and
three puncture wounds from heavy-gauge needles—one in my

right bicep from the PICC line, one on my right wrist from a cardiac catheterization, and one in my neck from the IV multiport monstrosity they gracefully refer to as "the Swan."

All ten of these wounds are in the process of being covered over with scar tissue. Once they are fully healed, they will be stronger than before. I find this to be poetic and more than a little satisfying. Watching them heal is fascinating. I do not ask my body to do this. It just does.

Why?

Because we were not meant to die. We were meant to live. That may sound absurd, given the fact that we all die. But I believe death is an intruder—the wage of sin[1] and an effect of living in a broken, fallen world.[2] I believe in a power greater than death, and I do not believe I am naïve to think this way.[3]

Suspicions about the wrongness of death are wired into us all. It is not a welcome presence. In my work as a pastor I spend time with many grieving people. One prevailing emotion they all seem to share is that the death of a loved one *feels* wrong—like it's not supposed to be this way. I agree with them, and I believe the way our bodies fight to recover when they have experienced something traumatic supports this notion that we were not meant to die, but to live.

My own experience supports this.

When I woke from surgery I was a mess. I had a broken sternum, a dead left foot, a malfunctioning brain, gallons of medications pulsing through my body, a puncture wound in my chest from the drainage tube, and the thick fog of sedation still hovering over me. Pain, confusion, immobility, and neurological short-circuits owned me in those first hours after waking up. I had never felt so fragile. I knew that my breastbone would fuse and the wounds would heal, but two days after surgery something happened that reminded me of just how vulnerable I am.

As I lay in my hospital bed sipping water, I felt the need to relieve myself. This was good news, the nurse told me, as she set a small plastic pitcher on my table. When we go through trauma, our brains, in order to conserve energy, go around to certain rooms of mental and physiological function and turn off the lights. Entire systems of our bodies more or less power down until we have the strength to resume our normal processes.

"So congratulations," the nurse said. "You have to pee!"

I asked my wife and parents to leave the room so I could have a little privacy. The container the nurse had given me was sitting on a table about two feet to my right, easily within my grasp. But when I tried to reach for it, I couldn't. The strange part of this was that I had not lost the use of my arm. I raised my hand and looked at it. I made a fist and then released it. I wiggled my fingers and then made them count to five. I raised my arm in the air and set it back down on my lap. I could perform all these tasks effortlessly. But when I tried again to reach for that pitcher, my brain refused to send that particular command to my arm. I could do everything else without a problem. I just couldn't reach for that container.

Once you promise your body that relief is coming, there are no take-backs. The longer I tried and failed to reach for that pitcher, the more urgently I had to go. In my desperation I called for help.

This act of calling for help highlighted another neurological problem. My request for assistance, I am told, came in the form of a profanity-laced tirade that would have made a comedian blush. I have no memory of this. It is funny to think back on that episode. I distinctly remember my panic. I remember feeling bewildered as I looked at my hand, which seemed to have a will of its own. I even remember calling for help. But I do not remember the blue streak that has now become the stuff of legend for my wife and parents. It seems I am a very creative cusser.

This vulgar verbal flourish was part of a temporary breakdown in my speech faculties. During the first forty-eight hours after surgery, when someone would ask me a simple question, sometimes I couldn't answer. When I meant yes, I would say no. When someone asked if I was thirsty, I would tell them I wasn't even though I was parched. I had a hard time remembering the names of everyday objects like my phone or the TV remote.

These complications were due to my neurological schism, sedation, the medications coursing through my veins, and the trauma of having my chest cut open. I was a weak, confused, frightened, and broken man.

〜〜〜

How did my body respond to all of this?

It fought. It fought immediately and with abandon. It fought like I was meant to live.

Within a matter of hours after discovering my paralysis, I was able to wiggle the toes on my left foot. Within a day, I could move my ankle. Over the course of three days, I went from being unable to sit up on my own to walking the hospital halls with a walker and a special boot. On the fourth day I ditched the walker, and on the fifth day I got rid of the boot.

My arms soon fell in line and began to obey my brain's commands. My answers to questions started representing what I was actually thinking. The five-inch scar down the middle of my chest began to heal, and the soreness in my throat from the breathing tube went away.

Are you impressed? Do you imagine the hospital staff gathered at the foot of my bed, staring at me, mouths agape, in awe of my progress? Well, they didn't. While they were certainly pleased, they were far from calling me a miracle. Why? Because my recovery was progressing precisely as they had expected. They had seen people like me bounce back like this a hundred times. They even told me before I went under the knife what the first five days of my recovery would hold, and they were more or less spot on. They said I would get exponentially better with each passing day. And guess what? I did.

How did my medical team know this would happen? They knew because this is what a body does when it goes through a traumatic ordeal. It fights to put itself back together as quickly as possible. The walls of my heart immediately began covering my internal stitches with scar tissue to strengthen what the surgeon's scalpel had weakened. My body began applying the nutrients from the food I had eaten to calcify the break in my sternum. My brain recognized the clot that caused my neurological event and instantly began to dissolve it before more damage could be done.

Even my pain has played a role. Pain is the body's way of enlisting our cooperation in the healing process. Had my natural curiosity led me to want to touch my scar, I could have infected it. But it hurt to touch, so I didn't. Even now, three weeks after surgery, it hurts when I try to use my upper body to push myself up out of a chair. That is because my sternum is still fusing together and doesn't want me undoing what it has accomplished so far. I have learned how to rely on my legs to stand up. Thankfully, my left foot has fully recovered.

———

Over the course of these past few weeks I have been living in a body at war with itself, and in my case healing seems to be winning. Sadly not everyone wins this fight in the flesh. That is part of our broken condition. Death comes for us all. But every person I have ever watched die has died fighting against it.

Even the weakest patient lying in a hospital bed fights against death in a host of ways. With every attempt to eat, we fight to supply our bodies with strength. With every fever, we fight against disease and infection. With every sensation of pain, we obey our limits as we feel the battle raging in our bones. We know that death does not become us.

Just as we were not meant to die, we were also not meant to be in pain. We were meant to be strong, glorious beings made in the image of God.[4] And we were not meant to be confused, though we all are. We were meant to be lucid; we were meant to understand who we are in relationship to our Maker and to his creation. I believe we long for this clarity of heart.

This world, as it stands, cannot satisfy our deepest longings. All it can do is sound the distant echo of another world—one where, though I die yet shall I live, and that by faith in the Son of God.[5] This is what we were meant for. Even as I watch my own body reassemble itself after such a great battle, I hear that distant echo of another world reverberating out of me—this bell that has been lifted and struck.

I marvel at the way my body is mending. It is such a mysterious process. Right now, I am physically very weak. I give everything I have to the process of recovery. There is no straight line to walk here. Healing can be a winding path with soul-crushing elevation gains and losses and more than a few false summits. Two steps forward, one step back. And yet, there is nothing for me to do but walk this path.

There is a simplicity to this stage of recovery that I enjoy. I rest. I eat and drink. I watch TV. I walk around the house and out to the mailbox. I take my medicine. I monitor my blood pressure and record the numbers on a chart for my doctor. I try to write. Beyond this, I don't do much else.

The lens through which I see my life right now is focused and small because it has to be. But my life will not always be this way. I will emerge from this stage of healing. I will begin cardiac rehab. I will go on longer walks. I will even run. My doctors will wean me off of my medications, and at some point I will return to work. I will go out to dinner with my wife. I will meet up with my friends for a movie or a concert. I will be clearheaded and able to read books again without forgetting what was on the previous page.

I know I will do all of these things. But one thing I will not do is return to the life I knew before I became sick. This affliction will not be a blip on the screen. I am in the process of changing. I have no idea what that change will look like, but I bear on my body the wounds of this travail, and I will carry those scars into whatever lies ahead. For the rest of my life I will see them when I stand in front of the mirror, and I will remember that I am changed. I am someone who has been broken and is being put back together.

Perhaps this is why I am developing an affection for my scars. In a strange way, they give me hope.

I do not know what changes lie further down the road. Right now, the task at hand is to heal. But as my body grows stronger, my mind and emotions will, at some point, step forward for their turn in line.

I cannot say for certain what my mental and emotional recovery will look like, but I sense a familiar storm gathering off in the distance. I feel it like an ache in my soul when the dark clouds begin to form. They are headed my way and will be here soon.

CHAPTER 9

MONSTER IN THE DARK

Depression

Two seasons were competing for the same ground. Spring struggling to be born. Winter struggling not to die. And it seemed to me some sort of parable. Was it a parable for me?

KEN GIRE

I am depressed.

My doctors told me this might happen—a detail my wife recently reminded me of when she saw the dark clouds rolling in. She has seen this in me before; we both have. I am no stranger to melancholy, despondency, and agitation. They have visited me many times. Still, even though being depressed is nothing new, this particular depression—because it is the one that rests upon me now—feels new. It always does.

My prior experience with this dark night of the soul tells me that, when unchecked, it has a tendency to become something untamable. And no matter how many times I've walked down this road, I still struggle to see it for what it is.

When a child hears a tapping on his bedroom window at night, until he turns on the light to see that it is only a branch blowing in the wind, it might as well be the knuckles of a dragon come to carry him off to its lair and lick his bones clean.

I know from experience that when I leave the voices in the dark unnamed, they become monsters. Tap. Tap. Tap. They try to persuade me to climb into their bubbling cauldron of my own volition. So in an effort to overcome the darkness, I am going to turn on the light the only way I know how: I am going to describe what I see and hear and feel, and then I am going to look into what winds are blowing that cause the tapping that has me so troubled.

This is what my depression feels like. This is my monster.

My depression feels like anxiety. Worry and fear are never far from me. When I am alone, my thoughts gravitate toward my burdens. When I lie down to sleep, my mind drifts to unresolved fears I cannot seem to shake. I worry—not about my present health, but about my future. Am I supposed to return to the life I knew before this affliction hit? Can I? The world I know—my friends, my work, my family—moves on while I sit in my recliner watching TV. The thought of climbing back into life feels overwhelming.

My depression also feels like grief over these seemingly wasted days. I lament that I spent my fortieth birthday and eighteenth anniversary in a hospital bed. It is the sort of sorrow I experience when I feel forgotten, which is a very unique sort of pain.

My depression feels like apathy. I do not care about things that once stirred me deeply. My desire to pastor people is all but gone right now. I don't want to listen to peoples' struggles—not because

I think theirs don't compare to mine, but because, search as I might for empathy, I honestly just don't care. This disinterest terrifies me. Will my compassion ever return? There are times when I cannot imagine it will, and that is a terrifying thought, which leads to another voice in the dark—futility.

My depression feels like futility. I cannot work. I cannot lift heavy objects. I cannot do anything that requires endurance or focus. I feel like I am wasting precious days—and, as Annie Dillard says, "How we spend our days is, of course, how we spend our lives."[1] I cannot concentrate. I can't hold a thought. I feel cooped up, deprived of sun and motion and warmth. I'm told exercise is great for keeping the depression at bay, but my best attempts at doing anything active reveal just how weakened I have become. This makes me irritable. My emotions are all over the map. Some days I cry easily. Other days I feel little if anything at all. This inability to reign myself in leads me to hopeless thinking.

So there they are—anxiety, grief, apathy, and futility. Anxiety raises questions about my future; grief casts a shadow over my past; and apathy and futility drape a fog over me in the present. These are my voices in the dark. This is the four-headed monster tapping on the window during the black night of my soul. He whispers his accusations into my ear, beckoning me to surrender hope.

You are letting people down. You are selfish. You have lost your spark. No wonder I feel so lost.

—————

There is no reasoning with the monster. Like the devil, he laces his lies with gilded threads of truth.

The truth is I am not yet recovered. I do depend on others to care for me. I wrestle with apathy, and sometimes it pins me to the mat. I have lost my spark. In my weakened state, this is where I am right now. This is all true.

In seasons like this, the straight truth is my best help. One truth my doctor told me early on was that this depression would probably find me after I had been home for a few weeks. And here it is, like a train pulling into the station right on time.

Now that I have named what I feel, I will describe what is actually happening to cause this tapping in the night. Why has this monster come to me now?

Depression is a predictable aftereffect of heart surgery. One common trigger is the anesthesia, which alters a patient's brain chemistry just enough to mix things up. Depression is also often triggered by postsurgery PTSD, or soreness and pain, or the extended neglect of care for one's well-being such as hygiene habits, exercise, or diet. It can also come as a side effect of antibiotics and other medications that have been introduced into the blood stream. I have experienced all of these triggers to one degree or another.

More medications course through my veins now than at any other time in my life. My nightstand is covered in pill bottles. Some of the pills help my body heal, but they also make me nauseated. For that, I take an anti-nausea medication which amps up my blood pressure. For that I take a blood-pressure medication which causes dizziness. Lucky for me, I'm taking that anti-nausea medication. Along with those, I take one pill to fight constipation and another to help me retain fluids when the anti-constipation medicine does its work.

And the painkillers. Oh, the blessed painkillers. I take a lot of oxycodone, as prescribed. Still, I get a few raised eyebrows when I tell people how much oxycodone I'm taking. I suspect I'm becoming chemically dependent on them, because when the pill bottle gets low I feel anxious.

What wonders those little pills are—reliable servants constantly eyeing the role of master. At some point soon I will step down from the narcotics, but for now my doctor tells me I must keep taking them because I cannot afford to devote any of my physical resources to dealing with pain. All my energy needs to go toward healing.

Together, all these medicines combine like a cocktail numbing my system.

As for my soreness and pain, they are less intense than they were. But it still hurts when I try to perform some of the most basic activities, like lying down or sitting up. Being unable to roll over without losing my breath is disheartening.

Then there's the lingering effects of the anesthesia. One doctor told me it can take roughly one month per hour of being under sedation to finally come out of the haze. I am foggy headed all the time. Writing is one activity I can do to keep my mind sharp, but it is hard work—a frustrating exercise in false starts, heavy revision, losing my way, editing, and taking my time.

Between the cabin fever, the effects of my daily meds, the pain, the loneliness, and the narcotics, I have begun to lose my grip on certain things I know, on an intellectual and theological level, to be true. When I pay attention to how I am feeling, I can almost see it happening.

This slide into sorrow has a name—depression.

If I am to see this depression for what it is, I need to remember what I have been through. My feelings come from somewhere. The scar down my breastbone and the puncture wound in my abdomen remind me that I have been through an ordeal. The reality is that I have been taken apart and reassembled. I am like a vase that has fallen and been glued back together; close inspection will reveal that I am not what I once was. I bear certain scars—inside and out.

My chest was opened up like a cabinet door, and parts of me that were never meant to see the light of day were held in a surgeon's hand. My heart was stopped for several hours as my blood passed through a machine. I experienced a strokelike neurological event that left me temporarily paralyzed and confused. The physical trauma I have experienced is both unfamiliar and significant.

Beyond the physical trauma, there's also the emotional weight. I have carried the burdens of facing my mortality for the first time and preparing for my own death. I have considered the possibility of unimaginable loss for my wife and children. I have prayed in advance for the grief they and my parents and friends might have known.

All these factors together make up the soil from which the seed of my depression has sprung. So what am I to do? I am to keep going—though, to be honest, some of the time I don't want to. One of the greatest lies the monster in the dark tells me is that I should neglect doing the things that I know on an objective level can only help—get good sleep, eat well, exercise, shower regularly, and nurture spiritual disciplines. I must avail myself of the means of grace that have been afforded to me—friendship, prayer, rehabilitation, Scripture, and time.

When I look objectively at the common symptoms people with depression tend to experience—change in appetite and sleep, irritability, hopeless thoughts, difficulty making decisions, and a general sense of apathy—I recognize that I own them all. The trick is to not let them own me.

This depression snuck up on me. It could easily have gone undetected, because in almost every other health-related area I am progressing nicely. My surgery was a success. My scars are healing, and my pain is decreasing. My heart sounds strong through the stethoscope. My murmur is gone.

But my mind and emotions are not recovering at the same pace as my body. That simple fact is very difficult to observe. And since post-op depression doesn't usually show itself until after the patient has returned home from the hospital, it can be difficult for family and friends, as well as the patients themselves, to understand what is happening.

Depression, when veiled by the good news of physical progress, hides beneath the skin out of earshot of the stethoscope, tapping on the window of my mind where only I can hear. It doesn't take much for me to feel alone and afraid in the dark. But when I turn on the light, here is what I see. On one hand, my depression is common enough that my doctor told me to watch for it. There are a number of factors that contribute to it—some are named, others are more mysterious. My body has been medicated, taken apart, and put back together.

But on the other hand, depression is not new to me. I've wrestled with it for years. It resides like a pox in my heart—dormant throughout much of my life, but able to be awakened nonetheless. And this reality is one I know I will live with long after my prescriptions run out and my body returns to normal and I go back to the routines of daily life. Knowing my own tendency toward melancholy makes me regard this particular season of depression as a sort of gift. This time around I feel like the monster is in a cage, like an old silverback gorilla at the zoo. I can observe him without too much fear.

This is a gift because I need to know this beast. I need to study his movements, watch what he responds to, and learn what calms him down because I know that unless the Lord chooses to remove this thorn from my side, I will continue to battle with seasons of depression. The time is coming when the monster will not be caged, and he and I will live together in the wild. He will lurk in the shadows, and I will try to train my senses to anticipate his ambush before he pounces.

But there will come nights, no doubt, when I will hear the tapping and my soul will be gripped with fear. By the grace of God, I will use what I learn from this season of depression to feel my way around the room to the switch, find the courage to flip it, and expose my depression in the light of truth.

Sometimes that light will be enough to deliver me from fear. But sometimes it won't. Such is the nature of the beast. God help me.

CHAPTER 10

CHARLIE AND THE MAN IN THE MASK

The Sacred Work of Rehabilitation

The blues is not your final judgment
It's no deep or evil power
Hey, the cure is very simple
And it works in half an hour
Get some sleep, eat some broccoli
Run a mile, take a shower
You're just down inside yourself.

DAVID WILCOX

God bless endorphins. If they had lips, I would kiss them.
Sitting in the tepid stew of my depression was about to do me
in when my doctor called to say I was ready to begin cardiac

rehab. Three times per week for three months I would go to the rehab facility for a supervised exercise regimen. I felt like a kid going to recess.

To celebrate, my wife and I went shopping. I got some new sneakers and workout clothes. I put together my gym bag and set it on the counter so I could experience the pleasure of looking at it. I had been cleared to exercise.

Sitting in depression can make an hour feel like a day and a day feel like a lifetime. Being able to get out of the house was itself a welcome diversion. But getting to exercise was cause for celebration. *Let's get the blood pumping. Let's take this new heart out for a test drive—open her up and see what she can do. Let's wake the endorphins and tell them there's a party. Thump. Thump. Thump.*

I cannot begin to express how much I looked forward to feeling the rush of exercise. Though I knew the facility was a simple rectangular building on the edge of the hospital's campus, I felt like I was headed to a five-star resort and spa.

The cardiac rehabilitation center is essentially a gym with cardio and weightlifting equipment. Nothing fancy. The difference is that the members of this gym are all in various stages of recovery from some major cardiopulmonary trauma.

My occupational therapist takes us on a tour and explains how the workouts will go. When I arrive, I am to go to the locker room and change into my activewear. Then I head over to a bank of battery-powered EKG receivers, stick three sensors on my chest, snap on the leads, power up the receiver, and report to the physical therapist, who enters the number on my receiver into her computer and then tells me what she would like me to do for the day.

The reason people come here is to do the work of rebuilding weak and broken bodies, minds, and hearts. We have our work cut out for us. Rehabilitation is a slow process with gradual gains. Many of us are used to being relatively strong, but when we climb on that treadmill on the first day of rehab, we discover that five minutes at a slow pace does us in.

There is no shame in this, however. We are all in the same boat. We are all here because we need help. We are a band of brothers and sisters, putting in the effort to rebuild what is broken.

Cardiac rehab is not how I imagined it would be. When my doctor first told me I would be doing this, I imagined a bunch of octogenarians on a bank of treadmills, and me waiting my turn for one to free up. I think I got this idea when he said it would be mainly heart patients—which I assumed was a condition relegated mostly to the elderly. And maybe also because that image made me laugh.

What I found is hardly what I imagined. There are many people here like me—first timers. We are relatively young, working to get back on our feet, confident we have what it takes to get there. We are eager and willing to be led. Just tell us what to do, captain. We'll make you proud.

Then there are the folks who have been through this more than once. I met a woman who has had four heart surgeries. She has been in and out of facilities like this for almost as long as I have been alive. These people are easy to spot—they are the ones with old scars. This isn't their first rodeo, and they are wise to the ways of this world. They smile at my enthusiasm but do not always share my optimism. I would not go so far as to describe them as discouraged, but their expectations concerning the quality of life they are working toward are measured and sober.

There is a young mom here who is playing the genetic hand she was dealt so that she can get back home to the suddenly sacred work of packing her kids' lunches, helping them with their homework, and tucking them in. She looks determined and resilient. I admire her. We all give her space.

Among the elderly, there are a couple of talkers—folks who like to stand in front of my treadmill and chat me up while I exercise. In any other circumstance this would annoy me, but I find that I enjoy the way they don't seem to take this too seriously. Their levity brings a nice balance to the gravity I know is in the room— gravity embodied by two different men I met, Charlie and the man in the mask.

〜〜〜〜

On my first day of rehab, I rode the elevator up with a man who was wearing a surgical mask. He was a complete enigma. He looked like a boy dressed in his father's clothes. His shirt hung loose on his emaciated frame. He wore a baseball cap two sizes too big for his head. It looked to be carefully balanced, as though one quick move would shake it off. He looked like a young teenage boy, except that peeking out from under his surgical mask was a full beard. I never heard him speak. He moved very slowly. There was a woman with him—maybe his wife, maybe his mother—who led him around by the arm so he wouldn't fall. I didn't need to know his story to know that whatever had happened to him, he had become a shell of his former self. He spent four minutes on a treadmill set to its lowest speed, and then he went home. I saw him two days later. He followed the same routine—four minutes, then home. I only saw him one other time after that.

Later that same week I met a man named Charlie at the EKG station. Charlie and I are the same age. I could tell when I met him that he had been at this for a while. He seemed to be back to his normal strength. He was friendly and talkative. He seemed to know most everyone there. When he told me he was almost finished with his rehab assignment, I saw a hint of nostalgia in his eyes—maybe even a bit of sadness. I asked if he had enjoyed his time in rehab. He had, very much. Charlie seemed like a man who enjoyed everything.

I had been told it was okay to ask people what brought them to cardiac rehab. People here don't mind telling their stories because we are survivors, and who doesn't like a survival story?

I asked Charlie, "What brought you here? Open-heart surgery?"

He replied, "Not exactly. I had a transplant."

"Wow. A heart transplant? Really?"

"Actually," he said, "I had a heart *and* lung transplant."

I suddenly felt a little starstruck. I needed to know more.

"Were the heart and lung from the same donor?"

"Heart and *two* lungs. And yes, they were from the same donor." Then he leaned in a little, smiled, and said, "And get this. The doctors put them in as a single unit." He tapped on his chest with his fingers like it was the hood of a classic car.

I didn't know what to say. *Who was this guy?* The breath-filled lungs and beating heart beneath Charlie's ribcage had been removed from another person, intact as a single unit, and placed into his hollow chest, and his body had received them. Amazing.

Charlie and the man in the mask stuck in my mind like counterparts of each another—wealth and poverty, power and frailty, life and death. The man in the mask moved about the facility like a wisp of smoke. He was translucent—like a ghost biding his time on the wrong side of eternity's door. But there was a certain grace in the way he moved, weightless, like he was already out of the earth's gravitational pull and drifting slowly toward another world. He had come to rehab to put on some pounds in the hopes that it might anchor him down here for a while longer. There was something sacred about him—angelic even.

Charlie, on the other hand, carried himself like a man who was getting away with something. Every time I saw him, he had this Mona Lisa smile on his face like he was savoring some clever inside joke none of the rest of us would get. I did not know Charlie before his surgery, but there had to have been moments in his life when he came close to fading into the shadowlands himself. He might have even looked like the man in the mask at one point. But here he stood, reborn and strong. He looked like resurrection—bright as Easter morning and as surprised as the rest of us that his tomb was empty.

～～～

I am nowhere near the two extremes of Charlie and the man in the mask, but I have come to a point in my recovery where what I decide to do next will chart my course. So I show up, put on my sneakers, stick the EKG leads on my chest, check in with my physical therapist, and do the work of recovery—me and the other survivors.

I have been working at this cardiac rehab for a while now, and I grow stronger every day. Rehab is a mysterious process. I cannot heal myself, but I can and must participate in that process. So I walk on a treadmill for an hour three times per week. I lift ridiculous little dumbbells. I do pull-ups on a machine that displaces most of my weight. These activities have expanded my lung capacity. They have helped my wounds heal and my sternum fuse. They have strengthened my atrophied heart. I am beginning to feel like myself again.

I regard cardiac rehab as a spiritual assignment. It is a spiritual task to put in the work of rebuilding a broken life. We are all either resisting or cooperating with the process of rehabilitation—physical and otherwise. There is something holy about taking up the task of stewarding a life, especially our own. If we come to this work at all, we must come with humble expectations and a willingness to be led. We submit to the process, trusting that the science is sound, even when what we're called to do hurts. The benefits of cardiac rehab far outweigh the pain. I am thankful for the progress I have made—and I still love the endorphins.

Along with my physical healing, I am also recovering emotionally. I suspect I will have some rehab work to do there as well. I am encouraged to discover that my appetite for community is returning. Cardiac rehab has helped reintroduce me into social situations.

I want to go out and get reacquainted with friends I haven't seen since I went down. But if I'm being honest, I am also nervous about that. I'm nervous because when I think of certain friends, my emotions go to a dark place and I don't know why. I feel wronged by friends who have only ever loved me. I cannot put my finger on why I feel wronged by them, but I can't deny that I do.

I have learned that this feeling of resentment is a relatively common experience for people who go through some kind of trauma that takes them out of their social lives for a season. We begrudge people for moving on with their lives while ours was brought to a halt. We struggle with jealousy over things we have missed out on that others have been able to enjoy—simple things like going to a movie or being invited to a party. We want the people around us to show us a satisfactory measure of genuine empathy, but no one has any idea what that looks like. This puts everyone in the precarious position of guaranteed failure.

I know that no one knows how to deal with stuff like this. There are no experts here. No one is sure how much they should reach out or how much space they should give. I haven't known how to advise them either. I don't know what to do with the feeling that some of my most treasured relationships are going to require a season of rehabilitation. If that is anything like cardiac rehab, it will be slow at first. But if we stay with it, I am confident our strength will return.

Emotional recovery is the part of this process no one really says much about. This part of rehab isn't as observable as watching scar tissue cover a wound or hearing a strong heartbeat through a stethoscope. What questions do you ask? What tests do you run? To what do you compare the present? It is difficult to measure emotional progress, and it is equally difficult to observe emotional decline. Both are nuanced. Both are subjective.

No one will make me do the emotional rehab. Few would even know to suggest it. I could neglect it and become like the man in the mask, emotionally gaunt and despondent, a shadow of my former self. Or I could take a page from Charlie's book and celebrate the fact that I am alive, that I have a new heart, and that I can begin again. I don't know if I can control the emotional outcome any more than I can the physical, but I can choose Charlie's path and try to walk in it. It will be a process, but that is the way I want to go.

CHAPTER 11

A TORNADO IN
A TRAILER PARK

Anger and Ego

Someone has altered the script.
My lines have been changed.
The other actors are shifting roles.
They don't come in when they're expected to,
and they don't say the lines I've written
and I'm being upstaged.
I thought I was writing this play . . .

MADELEINE L'ENGLE

A tempest has been building in my heart. It is like the pressurized stillness I feel before a thunderstorm rolls in. The air has a kind of weight to it.

As I work through cardiac rehab I see my strength returning. It is amazing how the body puts itself back together. But as I have put in the work of recovery, I've noticed a strange pattern: once one part of me begins to regain its strength, another facet of my brokenness steps forward for its turn in line. Is there no end? I honestly have no idea how long that queue stretches, but I suspect that I will never see this affliction as merely something from my past. I think it will always be, in one way or another, very present. Now I have to learn what to do with that thought.

One thing I know I must do is pay attention to what is going on not only in my body but also in my mind and heart, and right now my heart is fighting a war. I am angry.

It is in keeping with the human condition to want to find some reason for affliction. We utter nonsense like, "Everything happens for a reason." A cause, yes. A reason? I'm not always so sure. We look for healing, and we look for something or someone to blame. As we cycle through the stages of grief—denial, anger, bargaining, depression, and acceptance—we face the almost impossible task of trying to pin down what is true and then hold it there. But if I am going to steward the anger in my heart, I must try.

The truth is I am well loved. I have a happy home, a healthy marriage, and a clear sense of calling to the work I most enjoy. I have friends who believe the best in me and shoulder more of my burdens than I have ever asked them to carry. I am a man of faith— a worshiper in spirit and in truth. I am at peace with my Maker— prepared in the most essential ways to meet him. All of this is true.

However, none of this changes the fact that ego and grace are locked in a constant struggle for my heart. The voice of affection for the people in my life whispers into one ear, but incredulity at the ways they've failed me whispers into the other until the whispers become a roar, and that roar becomes a tempest that rips through my inner life like a tornado through a trailer park. I emerge after the storm and everything looks broken and scattered—a total loss. There is no clear line between my mess and the messes of those close to me. We are all caught off-guard. We are all confused. We are all stunned by how little it took to cause such a great catastrophe. We are poor in spirit, and the poverty we have shared this whole time is now on full display because of how easily everything was upended. We had no idea life was this fragile.

I vacillate between sorrow, self-pity, and numb indifference as my neighbors and I begin to sift through the wreckage together. Anger washes over me, and I lash out at whoever is close. I see a neighbor who never checked in on me and shout, "Where were you?" Then I wait for the warm sensation of vindication that never comes.

To another neighbor whose home remains miraculously untouched, I think to myself, *Of course. Nothing touches her.*

Then, from the corner of my eye, I see another neighbor wander over to where my bedroom used to be. This neighbor has a history of crossing sacred lines without invitation, and I am done dealing in subtleties. "Get off my property," I snarl, as if there remains anything he could possibly take from me now.

My heart is taking aim, and no one is safe. If I wanted, I could come up with reasons to be angry with everyone I know; there are sins of commission or omission I could hang on every last person in my life. I become angry when people smother me and when they leave me alone. I ruffle when family members tell the story wrong and when they ask me for clarity so they can tell it right. I resent the bacterial infection that started all of this. And ever since my doctor speculated that a recent dental cleaning may have been what introduced the bacteria into my bloodstream, I have regarded my dental hygienist as a criminal element.

The truth is I will never run out of people to indict. We are all guilty of so many failures to love well that if I wanted—and sometimes I do want—I could find some fault or transgression in everyone I know that I could then use to justify writing them off. I could blaze that trail to hell if I wanted to, and just the thought of it scares me.

What makes me want to blame my neighbors for the storm that hit us? Ego.

Blame is an exercise of the ego. It is the voice that tells me I do not deserve to be hurt or humiliated. When I think of affliction as humiliation, deserved or not, I cannot help but see it as something that "has been done to me." When this is my perspective, I want to know who afflicted me so I can know where to direct my rage. Often I direct it at my friends.

Friendship itself is a kind of affliction. I afflict my friends with the work of dealing with my shortcomings, my ignorance, and my vanity. I burden them and they burden me. Any friendship that is built on the value of never burdening one another is not much of a friendship. Burden-bearing is the essence of camaraderie. It is one of the holiest tasks one person can perform for another.[1] We were not made to thrive in isolation.

Ego calls all of that a lie. Ego demands that I stand alone as the hero of my own story. Heroes are strong. Heroes are needed but not in need. Ego seeks to place blame because I do not wish to appear weak, though I am. My ego is deeply offended by my affliction. Even as I write these words, my ego wants the world to regard me as some sort of guru because of my insights. This entire book might be the work of my ego attempting to cast me as a spiritual hero for the suffering. If it is, may God have mercy on my soul.

My recovery is shifting from a focus on my body to the healing of my mind, heart, and spirit. I stand in front of the mirror and see scars that will be visible for the rest of my life; I bear on my body the marks of my affliction. But my emotional, mental, and spiritual scars are harder to see. They do not bleed or swell. I am only just learning to know how to read their symptoms.

This war with ego and anger opens an emotional wound—a new facet of brokenness that steps forward and calls for my attention. I wish it didn't, but it does. I am not the first to face this struggle. Anyone who has suffered has heard their ego protest and felt their anger rise.

As I have tried to do with other parts of this unexpected journey, I will try to bring my ego and anger into the light. I will question them and attempt to listen for whatever truths might be hidden in their tantrums.

Here's a question: What if it was God who broke my heart?

I believe it was. Though I don't know all the reasons he brought this suffering on me, there are truths I know about God that lead me to believe my particular season of affliction comes from his hand and that it is for my good.

Historically, God deals with those he loves by breaking them. He leads people to the edge of themselves and then shoves them off into the unknown. He topples the towers to heaven we try to build. He confuses us to the point where we have to stop what we're doing and walk away because we can no longer carry on the work that once seemed so right and so clear.[2]

This is my God, the Divine Thwarter.[3] He is fiercely committed to opposing any attempts I might make to claim my independence

from him. It is because of his lovingkindness that he moves me
always deeper into a posture of dependence. Though I walk through
the valley of the shadow of death, I will fear no evil *because he is
with me.*[4]

I do not like being thwarted, but shall I receive good from God
and not also trouble?[5] The voices that say, *Recover so you can get back
to normal,* grossly underestimate the gift of this wrecked life. Why
is it a gift? Because I would have no compelling reason to step from
my comfortable existence into the quest for what's next if my
present security wasn't taken from me. It is rare for a man to plan
his own journey toward growth and change. Usually these journeys
are thrust on us unexpectedly. It seldom occurs to us to even consider them until the storm tears through and levels what we know.

If my ego tried to plan this journey, it would be limited by the
expectations of what I would already hope to find. There would be
no element of surprise, wonder, or faith—just a forced march
toward a future my present self assumes is what I need. That would
not be a journey of faith but of control—and a fool's errand. Faith
is the conviction to trust that there are good things out beyond
what I can see and would never know to pursue—glorious things
God himself will bring to pass.[6] I need those glorious things.

I also needed what God has brought. I needed to lose control. I
needed a broken heart. I needed to be dipped in the crucible of
suffering. Why? I may never fully know. But the God who brings
his children low does not do it for spite. He does it to awaken
desire, like a pang of hunger in the newly risen phoenix that makes
it unfurl its wings to fly. He does it to give us new eyes so that we
might see the world in a new light. He does it to stop us from
continuing down the path we're on and to set us on a new one. He
grants us weakness so that we might not trust too much in our own
strength. "Naked I came from my mother's womb, and naked shall

I return. The LORD gave, and the LORD has taken away; blessed be the name of the LORD."[7]

God deals in a sort of divine wisdom that often leaves earthbound creatures clueless. We emerge after the storm and cannot process the changes we see, but those changes send us down a road of renewal. We can be a good way down that road before we even know we're on it. What if the bacterium in my heart was a Father's wise and loving gift to his son? What if it was what C. S. Lewis called God's "severe mercy"—an act of love meant to return my heart to him by dealing a blow to my self-sufficiency?[8]

If my affliction was a severe mercy to awaken in me my need of God, then it is a wise gift from a loving hand. So then, what do I do with the anger that accompanies it? I wait for the fury to subside, and then I study what just came over me. When I do this, here is what I see: my initial flashes of rage are the way my heart rises to say I was not ready for this—like the surliness in a child just waking up.

The initial anger I experience is a response to the feeling of being suddenly disconnected from the life I knew. It is an animalistic reflex; I am a lion whose mane has been shaved, and I am looking for ways to make myself appear bigger. Untamed anger has the capacity to be a great danger to myself and others. I must pay attention to it. I must interrogate it. I must apologize for it when I hurt others with it. It is an open wound in my heart, and I do not know how long it will take to heal.

But even though it is untamed, my anger is anchored in something true. My anger is a protest against suffering. It is a groan for a life free from pain. It is an ache for the end of affliction and death.

To this I say to my anger, "Amen and amen," even though I know I must keep one eye trained on it, lest it rise up and consume me.

PART 3

LAMENT

MONTHS 6–22

CHAPTER 12

SEEING WITH
CLEARER EYES

Recognizing the Need to Lament

The exact same thing is never
taken away and given back.

C. S. LEWIS

Time is passing. The fog of my affliction has been lifting. As I begin to see with clearer eyes, I sense it will be crucial for me to lament what has happened. Lamentation is the intentional process of grieving and mourning so that we can bid an honest farewell to what we've lost and embrace the new identity our affliction has shaped for us. I don't feel defeated or depressed anymore, but I sense in my heart a rising importance to grieve and mourn what I've been through.

I am praying for eyes to see and ears to hear, but my emotional presence remains muted under the influence of the shock of my sudden affliction in much the same way that my mind has remained clouded because of the narcotics in my system.

~~~~~

During a recent hospital visit, my doctor asked how I was feeling. I told him how every night I would sit in my chair in the living room, shifting continually, agitated and restless, until I couldn't take it anymore.

"Good night, everyone," I would announce and head off to bed.

After a couple of weeks I realized this had become a nightly occurrence. Without fail, sometime between seven thirty and eight, this feeling of general irritation would come over me. Five months had passed since surgery; my wounds had long since healed, and I was nearly done with cardiac rehab, but I could not shake this discomfort.

As I explained, my doctor began to nod his head.

"That is called dysphoria," he explained.

"Dysphoria?"

"Yes. You've heard of euphoria? Dysphoria is the opposite. You have a general feeling of being unwell, right? You don't ache in any one particular place, but you can't seem to sit still or get comfortable, and you just kind of feel bad all over?"

"Yes, exactly," I said. "What is that?"

"Well," he said, "you are addicted to narcotics."

"I am *what?*"

He said, "You are addicted to painkillers."

Then he reminded me of a conversation I had with my surgeon the week before they opened me up. My surgeon had explained, "When you come out of surgery, your body is going to pour every ounce of energy you have into healing. You must cooperate with this process. If you allow yourself to be in pain, you will begin to do things that will slow your body's healing. You will sit funny in your chair, which will make your back hurt, which will make you uncomfortable when you sleep, which will wear you out and make you even more sore and restless the next day. All of that requires energy you can't afford. If you decide you are going to be a hero and try to tough this out by not taking your pills, you will end up working against the healing process. So you need to take these meds. Take them as prescribed, but take them."

I gave him my word that I would follow his orders.

"One thing you need to know," he said. "Oxycodone is highly addictive. If you take the dose we are going to prescribe, you will most likely develop some chemical dependency. We will deal with that if and when it comes. But you have to take the pills. Understand?"

That was how I climbed aboard the Oxycodone Express. She is a fast train—so fast that it is hard to keep track of what's going on as the world flies past. But boy is she smooth. Luxuriously smooth. I rarely felt a thing. And when I did, I didn't care. It has been a nice ride, but I boarded that train back in early summer and now, months later, my conductor was telling me it was time to come down.

So there I was, an accidental drug addict in the throes of detox and withdrawal. As a person who had never used illicit drugs, the impact of my doctor's words surprised me. I felt no fear, shame, or guilt—only fascination. *So this is drug addiction?*

There are men and women I admire whose lives have been turned upside down because they developed a dependency on the same pills I was taking. I could see how easy it would be to end up there myself. I couldn't play around with this.

Addiction demands things of us and then plays dirty to get them. Addiction saunters into our lives, saying, "I can help you feel good." But before you know it, the pill bottle is running the show from behind a big mahogany desk you don't recognize, saying, "Now stay with me if you don't want to feel bad." That is where the deepest trouble lies. It is not simply that I want to feel good. It is that I do not want to hurt, and that is a very powerful desire. It would be very easy for me to lose my way.

Coming down is no simple matter. My doctor explained that the restlessness came over me at around the same time every night because even though I had scaled back to only one oxycodone in the evening, my body still clamored for that pill. The routine was stamped onto my brain. *It's time for the pill, so how about we take that pill?*

I asked my doctor, "Should I stop taking it?"

"No, no," he said. "I want you to break that pill in half for the next five days, and then half again for another five. You need to come down carefully. There are potential complications with quitting cold turkey that your body may not be able to handle."

I followed his instructions and successfully weaned myself off the narcotics. The process felt a little like waking up—moving from the "anything goes" world of dreams, through the space between sleep and awake, to at last planting my feet on the ground and standing up. As time passed, I became more alert. I began to see the world with clearer eyes. As the narcotic fog burned off, I turned my attention to the work of bidding an honest farewell to what I had lost as I faced the new identity my affliction shaped for me.

During this season, I spent time with my friend Barbara. She had gone a couple of rounds with cancer, and it had returned. Sometimes, after my rehab and her radiation, we met at a cafe to talk.

Barbara and I knew who we were to each other—friends, believers in Jesus, and survivors. When we met, we compared notes on our procedures, our drugs, our progress, our setbacks, and our spiritual lives. Barbara was strong. Scripture poured out of her when she talked—the overflow of what she had hidden in her heart from years of walking by faith.

During one of our coffees, I told Barbara how I sensed the nearness and goodness of God in the midst of my suffering. I didn't question his goodness or his love, I told her, and I felt that this travail had somehow strengthened my affection for him and revealed more of his love for me.

Barbara said, "I had a very similar experience when I was first told I had cancer. The Lord seemed so close, and though I did not always understand, I trusted him implicitly. It was a holy time. You don't know how you are going to respond to suffering until you are in it. The peace I felt was so clear."

Then she paused. "I do not feel that way this time," she said. "I believe God loves me. I believe he is good. But right now I have a lot of questions and a few complaints. I don't know why this time around feels different, but it does. When I was first diagnosed I was accustomed to feeling invincible. I was determined that I would fight this cancer and that I would win, and that is exactly what I did. After surgery, chemotherapy, and losing my hair, my cancer went into remission. But now it is back, and I am confused. I don't understand why God is doing this. I really don't."

This was the voice of lament. In the Bible, a lament is a complaint bound to faith, confusion bound to trust, and petition bound to allegiance.[1] For Barbara, the frustration she felt and her trust in God did not contradict one another. Her vow to praise him was not contingent on how he responded to her petition for help. She prayed to him because she believed he was deeply involved in her life even though she didn't understand what he was doing. She appealed to him because she believed he had the ability to help. She complained to him because she trusted that he loved her and wanted good things for her.

Barbara had time to sit with her sorrow. She had time to not only grieve over her cancer but also to begin the work of mourning—entering into that active process of letting go of the relationships, dreams, and routines her cancer had either changed or taken from her.

I was the rookie, full of the same invincibility Barbara felt her first time around. I believed I would emerge on the other side of my suffering better than before, and that was exactly what I was doing. Her vulnerability humbled me. Affliction is not some test that simply exists to build our character. It beats us up. It changes us. It sobers us. It raises ultimate questions. After listening to Barbara's honesty, I wondered if I had been making some sort of game out of my own suffering—like it was a test to pass or a book to write or a story to tell at church.

This is sacred business—the fragility of life. Barbara wanted me to respect that. She wanted me to acknowledge it. Here was a woman who loved her Lord. She really did. But she had some questions she wanted him to address, even though she knew she could not demand that God give an account of himself. Barbara wanted to know why God allowed suffering. Was it spiritual warfare? Was it a trick of the devil? Was it somehow a way to serve God, and if so, had he ever considered how that would look to us? These are all questions of lament.

Her honesty sobered me. In the same way that my doctor walked me down from my oxycodone fog, Barbara walked me into the realm of honest lamentation.

My friend Jaco teaches on the importance and power of lament. He says it is a vital part of our recovery.[2] How so? Lament freely acknowledges the limitations of living in a broken body in a fallen world while affirming the value of both. It grants us permission to protest the sorrows over which we grieve. It empowers the weak and vulnerable by giving us something constructive to do with our pain. It prepares us to think in new ways about ourselves and about God. It affirms our responsibility to care for our own hearts. It brings our anger and desire for satisfaction under the scrutiny of truth, rather than letting them run wild. It facilitates fellowship and understanding with other sufferers. It creates a context for us to honestly express genuine praise and hope. And it moves us through the process of mourning while honoring the fact that this process takes time and leads us to insights we have yet to gain.

I do not yet understand the full scope of my grief. I know this. For this reason, I need to lament. As Jaco describes it, I need to "complicate" my grief by engaging in the work of exploring all the loss and change that has come my way. The more I work at it, the more I come to understand the loss over which I now grieve and mourn.

I have experienced relational change. My affliction sidelined me for a season from much of my community. Though my friends and family have loved me well through this process, their lives have continued on in my absence, and I feel that loss as a sorrow. I mourn over not being able to share experiences with them, and over them not being able to share this life-altering experience more with me. In my darkest moments, I missed the emotional and physical presence of those who love me.

I've also endured a functional loss. I lost my body for a time. When we're healthy, we take for granted how much the use of our bodies contributes to our emotional health, the development of our relationships, and the nurturing of a marriage. But for a few months, I lost the ability to physically function, and it has felt in many ways like lost time.

I also lost my mind. The medication made it virtually impossible to read with any sort of retention. Often, I could not recall what I had read just two pages ago. My short-term memory was spotty at best. (Did I already say that?) I struggled to remember peoples' names. On one occasion I lost all memory of a meeting I had with a couple whose wedding I had agreed to perform. I couldn't remember their names, which was bad enough. But two weeks after meeting with them, I had absolutely no memory of that appointment. I found a full page of notes I took from our time together, but I could not remember writing them. I still don't. Seeing that page written in my own hand was unnerving, like receiving a letter from my future self.

I have had to deal with the realities of mental lapses and the prospect of permanent cognitive decline. This feels a bit like I'm losing my self—and I grieve not only over the prospect but also over the fact that, at some point in my life, losing my mental acuity will certainly happen. This affliction has given me a taste of the decline that comes for us all.

I also lost my role. We live our lives in specific social relationships and networks. These roles dictate much of how we spend our time (going to work, leading Sunday services), where we physically spend our days (at an office, in a school, in a particular city block), and who we are in relationship to others (pastor, coworker, friend who is invested in a present struggle). My affliction interrupted how I function in my various roles, and I know it will take some time to get back up to speed.

If I wanted, I suppose I could write these losses off. But there is a stored up sorrow in my heart—one I can feel—and I want to let it out. To let it out, it must run through me. I want to name my sorrows, feel them, acknowledge the losses and changes they have brought, and mourn them in order to better understand the way my affliction has changed and shaped my life as I move forward. And I want to do this before the face of God.

It is spring now. I'm nearing the one-year anniversary of the fever that started all this. A couple of weeks ago Barbara came over to help my wife and I paint our kitchen. She moved gingerly, like she was in pain. She told us her back hurt and that it was hard to breathe. Her husband John took her to the doctor, who ran some tests and took some images. The results were not good. Her cancer had spread. It was everywhere. The doctors gave her less than one week to live.

CHAPTER 13

BARBARA

Returning to the Work
of Burden Bearing

Gentlemen of the city, what surprises you?
That there is suffering here, or that I know it?

ANNIE DILLARD

You better put down that stone."

"What do you mean? What stone?" John asked.

"That stone in your hand," Barbara said.

John looked at his wife, and then at the crumpled up napkin he was holding. He looked at her again to see if she might be making a joke, but all he saw on her face was a look of earnest concern.

"Barbie, this is just a piece of paper. See, I don't have a stone," he told her, showing her the napkin.

She looked confused. John could see the beginnings of the cognitive dissonance the doctors said would creep in. She was starting to drift.

One week earlier Barbara had gone to the hospital because she was having trouble breathing. This was on a Saturday. Her medical team ran tests and took pictures of her lungs. What the doctor saw on those images was enough for her to decide not to show them to John. Instead, she took him aside, explained that Barbara's cancer had spread, and then she told him Barbara had maybe three days to live.

The next morning when Barbara woke up in her hospital bed, John said, "Barbie, I need you to listen to me. It's not good. The doctor says this is serious. You may only have three days."

John told me her expression was that of a confused angel.

Through her oxygen mask, she said, "But John, I prayed. That's not what Jesus told me."

Word quickly made its way around to her friends and family. I drove to the hospital as soon as I could. A dozen people gathered in the hall, waiting their turn to go in to see her. The hospital staff told us we needed to go to the waiting room so we wouldn't clog the halls. Barbara was very tired. John thanked us all for coming and sent almost everyone home so his wife could get some rest. Then he told me that if I wanted to go in, Barbara would be glad to see me.

I retrieved my Bible from my car, went into her room, and stood by her bed. She looked at me and said hello as she drifted in and out of sleep. I asked if she would like for me to read to her. She nodded.

I turned to the Gospel of John and read, "In the beginning was the Word, and the Word was with God, and the Word was God. He was in the beginning with God. All things were made through him, and without him was not any thing made that was made. In him was life, and the life was the light of men. The light shines in the darkness, and the darkness has not overcome it."[1]

She asked me to read on, so I did. I read to her about the Lamb of God who takes away the sins of the world.[2] I recounted how Jesus transformed water into wine at the wedding in Cana, and how this was a foreshadowing of Christ's own wedding yet to come.[3] I told her, "God so loved the world, that he gave his only Son, that whoever believes in him should not perish but have eternal life."[4] We met the woman at the well, whose life was hard, and who wanted to drink from Jesus' living water, and the official from Capernaum, whose son Jesus healed with only a word, and that from a great distance.[5] I read about how Jesus asked the lame man by the pools of Bethesda if he wanted to be healed,[6] and how Jesus said that if people wanted fellowship with him, they would have to eat his body and drink his blood, and how the people found this teaching to be deeply offensive. Many of Jesus' followers turned away after hearing this. But when Jesus asked his disciples if they would also leave, Peter said, "Lord, to whom shall we go? You have the words of eternal life."[7]

Jesus had a way of beckoning followers through great displays of divine power, but then only meting out that power when it seemed wise to him. Anyone who has ever truly followed Jesus has followed *this* Jesus—the one who can heal with only a word but doesn't always choose to do so.

When I finished John 7, Barbara was sound asleep. I closed my Bible, kissed her on the forehead, and left.

In typical Barbara fashion, she stabilized, and on the following Saturday they sent her home. Though her vital signs were improving, the doctors warned us that her scans told a different story. Her condition grew worse by the day.

Back at home, John and other family members and friends took turns caring for her and their kids. We brought meals, notes, and gifts for the family. We helped run errands and clean the kitchen.

Barbara lay in a bed provided by the hospice center. I stopped by to see her as often as I could. She fought, but she was slipping. She made it through the weekend, but on Monday, Barbara was complaining about discomfort. John knew that for Barbara to verbalize her pain it had to be pretty bad. She was tough. So she went back to the hospital.

As the doctor gave John, Barbara, and Barbara's sister her best explanation for what was going on, Barbara looked at her husband and sister and said, "You two have got to stop loving me so much and let me go." This was new. Barbara had not spoken like this before.

John took Barbara home. When they pulled up into their driveway, John came around to the passenger side, lifted his wife from her seat, and danced her from the car into the house. He told me this was something they had done on occasion—a secret language of love known only between this husband and wife. They felt joy—a sweet embrace in the midst of a dark time. He danced her all the way to her bed, where he laid her down and tucked her in.

———

The next morning, I stood in their kitchen and saw a painting hanging on their wall that read, "In this world you will have trouble. But take heart. I have overcome the world. John 16:33." I asked John where they got it. He told me it had been given to Barbara when she first was diagnosed. Ever since then, the painting had hung in a prominent place so they would all see it and remember.

I went in to see Barbara, but by this time she could no longer speak. John sat beside her and talked to her, but none of us knew whether she could hear us. I kissed her again on the forehead and left them alone.

That Tuesday afternoon, as John sat at the desk in their bedroom going over some paperwork, Barbara looked at him and said, "Hey, baby."

This was something Barbara said often to her friends and children. But when she said it that afternoon, John told me she said it in a different way. She said it as a lover and a wife. Those two words carried the intimacy of more than two decades of marriage.

"Hey, baby" were the last words she spoke.

Early the next morning, at 4:00 a.m. that Wednesday, Barbara took her last breath.

I drove to their house as soon as I got the news. I went in to see Barbara one last time before the funeral home came and took her away. After that, I sat with John to help him begin the difficult task of making her arrangements.

We secured a church for her memorial service and made a rough outline of how that service would go. Then he and I, along with one of Barbara's brothers, drove to the funeral home and cemetery to purchase her casket, burial plot, and grave marker. A funeral home employee drove us around in a golf cart and showed us various examples of headstones and empty plots from which to choose. As a pastor, I had been through this process before. Still, it was a strange experience looking through catalogs of caskets and headstones and being appraised of the special features of the higher-end models. I understand that these decisions must be made, but making them causes my heart to cry out, "Come, Lord Jesus."

After making our selections, John asked if I would come back by the house and prepare their kids for the visitation on Friday night and the memorial service on Saturday. A familiar strength rose up in me—the fortitude of burden bearing. Barbara was honoring my life by calling on me to officiate the celebration that marked the end of her suffering. It had been a while since I had stood on such sacred ground, and it occurred to me that her funeral marked a certain milestone in my own recovery. I was now returning to the work of bearing the burdens of others—work I had been unable to do only months before.

That Friday night, people came from all around to pay their respects to Barbara and her family. I monitored the traffic flow and ran interference to make sure John and the kids were able to slip away into the greenroom to rest, grab a bite to eat, and get a respite from the crowd. I felt proud of the way Barbara's family endured this difficult task with such grace.

Then on Saturday morning, we gathered at the church for a short memorial service, after which we drove out to the cemetery. John and I had arranged for the funeral director to lower Barbara's casket into the ground during the graveside service so that John and the kids could lay roses over her burial vault and each pitch in a handful of dirt as a way of saying goodbye.

Once Barbara's casket had been placed on the lowering straps and I had finished my brief graveside service, committing Barbara's body to the earth and her soul to the care of her Maker, the funeral director whispered something to John. No one could hear what he said, but John nodded and whispered something back, pointing to the hand crank that lowered the casket.

Without taking off his suit coat, John knelt in the dirt beside Barbara and began to turn the crank himself. The way the gears aligned made it so that each revolution only lowered the casket about half an inch. John turned that crank again and again. The work was hard and slow. Sweat beaded on his forehead. His friends and family watched in reverence as he carried out to the end the vows he made to his wife on the day they married. Inch by inch, turn by turn, death slowly parted them as a husband lowered the body of his wife into the ground. John did not stop until her casket rested safely on the floor of the burial vault. Then he gathered his children, and they each cast a rose down into the earth's open wound. The grave workers then lowered the vault's concrete lid, which seated itself with the heavy sound of permanence.

———※———

C. S. Lewis, in *A Grief Observed*, wrote about how people would attempt to comfort him after his wife died by saying, "She is in God's hands now." Lewis described his grief as a wound given to him by God and then he described his wife's death as the sword God used to cut him open. Lewis wrote, "'She is in God's hands.' That gains a new energy when I think of her as a sword. Perhaps the earthly life I shared with her was only part of the tempering. Now perhaps he grasps the hilt; weighs the new weapon; makes lightning with it in the air. 'A right Jerusalem blade.'"[8]

The Lord used Barbara to cut open the hearts of many. Though I did not know her nearly as well as many others, I am one of them.

As I watched John lower that casket, something broke inside of me—like the release of the chains that hold an ocean liner in dry dock until she is ready to be set adrift. I felt a hibernating sense of purpose come awake. As I looked at his family and at the crowd that had gathered, I considered my role as the officiate of this unfolding drama and I remembered who I am. I am a pastor. I shepherd people's hearts. This is what I do.

Healthy mourning eventually requires us to not only receive acts of compassion but also to give them. It was a holy honor to care for that family in their hour of need. I had spent the better part of the year mostly on the receiving end of help. This funeral, one year after my affliction, was a significant part of my healing. The Lord used Barbara to lift me up from my season of dependence on others so that I might be depended on in a time of great need. I am grateful to Barbara for that, and to the Lord.

CHAPTER **14**

A SONG OF LAMENT

A Year of Grappling with Suffering Before God

You who have made me see many
troubles and calamities will revive me
again; from the depths of the earth
you will bring me up again.

PSALM 71:20

It has been one year since Barbara died and two years since
my heart surgery. I have had a lot of time to think. I have walked
through rehabilitation, depression, anger, chemical dependency,
lamentation, and the death of a friend. Every step of this journey,
whether I've known it or not, has been a procession to the feet of
my Lord. I have brought him my fever, my fear, my convalescence,
my pain, my sorrow, and my uncertainty.

Suffering awakens all sorts of sleeping giants—timidity, self-pity, bitterness, a sense that something unfair has happened. The apostle Peter told early Christians not to be surprised when they faced trials of many kinds, as though something strange were happening to them. He told them to entrust their souls to their faithful Creator.[1] I believe this charge also applies to me.

Of course, Peter's admonition is nothing new in the pages of Scripture. Well over three hundred times the Lord tells his people not to fear, and follows that command with the reason why: because he is with them.[2]

If suffering should not come as a surprise, and if our comfort is found in the promise of the nearness of God, that means the furnace I have been in is the furnace he has chosen for me.

Here in the furnace I offer my song of lament.

Lord, you are with me. We walk through the valley of the shadow of death together.[3] Since I do not know the way, I have no choice but to trust you. To trust you means I walk a steady path believing you are with me. The sound of my footfall echoes the two operative words you use to call us to the communion table—remember and proclaim. I remember that you are a Man of Sorrows, acquainted with grief, and I proclaim that I have no better guide.

I have no better guide for two reasons: because you are God and because no one else has stepped forward to lead me in a worthy manner. So I follow. What else can I do?

~~~

I must remember that God does not owe me a life free from suffering. To expect that he does is to grossly misread the Scriptures. Pick a saint, any saint, and you will find a trail of sorrow, hurt, sin, and catastrophe in their wake.

Behind Abraham sits Hagar a bowshot away from her son Ishmael who has been cast out of the camp. She is waiting for the boy to die.[4]

Behind David is Uriah the Hittite lying dead on the battlefield while the king's son grows in Uriah's wife's womb.[5]

Behind Peter, the sound of the cat o' nine tails raking across the back of his best friend is interrupted by the crow of a rooster.[6]

The Lord does not owe me a pain-free life. But he does promise to be with me in it.

Because the Lord often withholds explanation for our pain, we must not look at suffering as though it is some divine gimmick designed to teach us some important life lesson. That would make too little of the reality. God's people do not walk through suffering toward the moral of the story. Rather, we walk toward the eternal presence of the Maker and Lover of our souls. This I must remember.

I must also proclaim that "it is a fearful thing to fall into the hands of the living God."[7] Suffering is not an event. It is a path. Scripture calls it a road pocked with miry clay and slippery rocks.[8] There are plenty of advisers out there who would counsel me to dress this up in positive thinking. But I do not think it would be honest to try to pad my experience with cleverly contrived optimism that denies what is true. My faith in Christ provides a deeper, truer way. I want to feel my sorrow. I want to walk in it. If the Lord walks there with me, what possible advantage could there be in conjuring another way?

No, I choose the road of suffering, and I pray for the courage to walk it honestly. The truth is my heart is broken. I need time to say as the psalmist said, "When I remember God, I moan; when I meditate, my spirit faints."[9] As part of my confession of faith, I need to say that I am not okay—not completely.

Lamentation is a part of worship. It is that part of us that cries out over the sorrow of the suffering, pain, and relational brokenness by which we have all been hurt. I lament to the Lord that over these past two years I have been the bruised reed he has promised not to break.[10] I am the smoldering wick he has promised not to extinguish. I am the brokenhearted whose wounds need binding.[11] God gave me this body with all of its physical limits, and then he broke me. He is at the same time my Healer and the one who has permitted my affliction.

Like Barbara, the deeper I venture into this affliction, the more questions I have. But I remember C. S. Lewis who said, "When I lay these questions before God I get no answer. But a rather special sort of 'no answer.' It is not the locked door. It is more like a silent, certainly not uncompassionate, gaze. As though he shook his head not in refusal but waiving the question. Like, 'Peace, child; you don't understand.'"[12]

I have reconciled myself to the fact that there is much I do not understand. But where else can I go? He alone has the words of life.[13] Though he slay me, yet will I trust him. But though I trust him, yet shall I lament that he has slain me.

—————

The fear in me wants to call foul on this whole business of looking to this often-silent God for comfort. But here is the thing about the silence of God: he is never utterly silent. He may chose not to answer my questions as I have framed them, but he has addressed the heart of my issue at great length. The immutable God has shown himself faithful across the globe and down through time. Who am I to presume that my case is the one for which he will alter his course?

In affliction I gain a greater perspective of my deep need of him, but I also see more of his grace as a result. I am like the apostle Peter who leapt out of the boat on that morning after the resurrection and swam to the feet of the friend he had denied. Why did Peter do this? Because though he had denied knowing Jesus in his greatest hour of need, the truth remained that Peter loved his Lord. He was a living contradiction, just like me.[14]

When Jesus asks his sopping and sorrowful friends if we love him, it is because he wants us to hear ourselves speak the truth. We do. I do. God help me, I fail him, but I do love him.

This is the nature of my relationship with God, which means I can trust him even when I do not understand him. I can trust that he is not distant or sleeping. I can trust that he is working in ways I cannot see, and unto ends I cannot predict. What I can see, however, is that God has used suffering and affliction in the lives of his people to bring amazing things to pass. With that, I must also remember that only some of his people get to see what he is doing before he calls them home.

Even though God owes me no explanation, historically he has said much. One thing God has said is that his power is made perfect in our weakness.[15] I may not see all there is to see about my season of affliction, but what I have seen—these stories I have told, these matters with which I have wrestled, this heart I have interrogated—would not have happened if I had not been lifted and struck.

So I, a weak and complicated disciple, limp alongside the God of all eternity. And I cry as I follow. I avail myself of the help he has given—prayer, Scripture, friends, time, the local church, medical professionals, drugs, and words. When I look at that list, I remember again just how weak I really am.

Though I continue to ask why, more often than not the question on my mind is "What's next?" Sometimes he will answer, sometimes he will not. And I will again have to lean on what I know of who he is when I cannot make sense of what he allows.

This, at its core, is what it means to follow the Lord. Though I do not always understand him, Christ is calling me to something very real; he is calling me into obedience. I am learning how to obey the Lord, not for the clarity of the reward he will give if I would only come to him, but because the one who calls is faithful.[16] I deprive my own heart of savoring the goodness of God when I demand that I see my reward before considering whether or not I will follow him.

The Lord must be the object of my faith. Part of walking with God means confessing that he alone is God, and if he is, then he alone is worthy of my obedience and worship. I will not find rest for my soul in any other place. God has not been silent. He is not unknown to us. So I will ask him for the grace to remember his faithfulness down through the ages, and for the humility to not imagine that I would be the one to bring that faithfulness to its end.

***

I am grieving the loss of the life I knew before I fell ill. I grieve my inability to have stopped it, and the difficulty it caused for those who love me. I have watched my thirteen-year-old son set aside some of his innocence so that he might take up the role of being another man in our home. I have watched my daughters treat with delicacy the daddy they used to climb all over, lest they hurt me. I have watched my wife carry our household with dignity and strength as a single parent. She fed me, filled my prescriptions, made my bed, and cared for our children because she made a vow to love me in sickness and in health. All of this arouses a deep and holy sorrow.

I am not the same person I was. I think about my own loss of innocence—about the seriousness that has come over me since I fell ill. I am not without humor—not by any means—but I have walked through the valley of the shadow of death, and I have changed. Though my body has physically healed, I am still recovering in other ways and always will be.

This makes me wonder about my future. Has God introduced something that will radically change the direction of my life? Has he only just begun? For the time being, the Lord, as a way of loving me, has limited my capacity for the emotional and physical stamina much of what I do to provide for my family requires. I receive these limits from his hand, but I do not know what they will mean for my future.

The irony is that this path I walk feels like it is leading me not toward a grander complexity of life but toward a greater simplicity. Though this world is complicated with brokenness and evil, it was established by a Maker who said of it, "This is very good."[17]

And good remains here. I know it does. I see it all around me. This is part of my lament. I taste the goodness of the Lord, but I also taste the sorrow of affliction. I ache for the renewal of all things, and I pray for the grace to continue to follow my Shepherd through the valley of the shadow of death, trusting that he prepares a table for me in the presence of my enemies, that goodness and mercy shall follow me all the days of my life, and that I shall dwell in the house of the Lord forever.[18]

Joy comes, but now is the time for tears. May the one who made my heart and broke it accept my lament as part of my worship.[19]

May he comfort me and give me gladness in exchange for my sorrow.[20] May the One who has stripped my soul clothe me with joy.[21] And may the words of my mouth and the meditations of my heart be pleasing in his sight.[22]

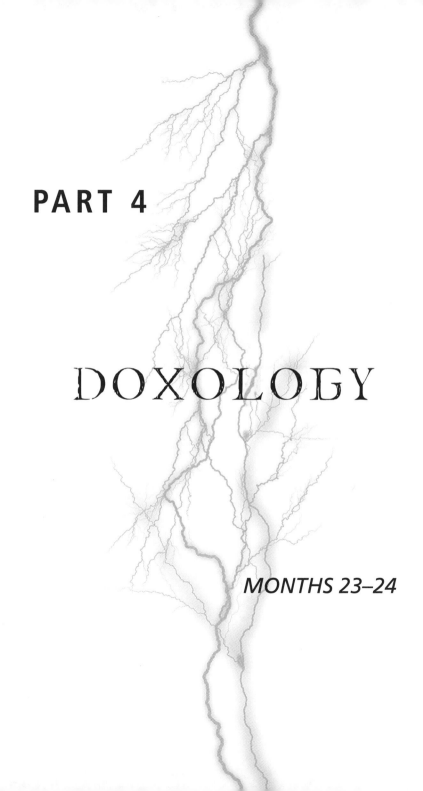

PART 4

DOXOLOGY

MONTHS 23–24

CHAPTER 15

TO CLIMB A MOUNTAIN

Finding a Way Forward

When an old man dies,
a library burns to the ground.

AFRICAN PROVERB

Twenty years ago when I married Lisa, I did not know her. And she did not know me. We were two. We were kids just out of college. I was twenty-two and she was twenty-one. Neither of us knew much about life outside of the nest. But we knew we wanted to figure it out together—the two of us.

Four children, three cities, and twenty years later, she and I woke up beside each other in Keystone, Colorado. It was 4:00 a.m. We got dressed and laced up our hiking shoes, I loaded a small backpack with water and snacks, and we drove into the Tenmile Range to the Quandary Peak trailhead. On our twentieth anniversary—two years after my open-heart surgery—she and I set out to summit a fourteen-thousand-foot peak. It would be her first fourteener and my seventh, which meant I would lead us because I was the one who truly knew what we had gotten ourselves into.

The Quandary Peak trail is relatively easy, as far as fourteeners go. It requires no technical equipment or mountaineering experience. But the terrain itself is not where the challenge lies. The most difficult part of a climb like this resides in the space between our ears. The mental ascent seems much higher than the physical one.

We parked at the trailhead, stretched, and began to climb. Soon we fell into a line of hikers winding our way through the pine and aspen, following the trail first by the light of the moon and then by the rising sun.

The thrill of the adventure and the beauty of the mountains got us out of bed, but I had told her about how when the air gets thin it becomes difficult to think straight. We would have to be strategic in the way we thought about the journey ahead. I knew that when we caught our first glimpse of the summit, we would feel a mix of awe and dismay—awe at the thought of reaching that glorious height, dismay at the thought of what it would take to get there.

When it gets hard to breathe, it becomes difficult to keep moving. By the time we saw the summit way off in the distance we were already exhausted, and our legs felt heavy as concrete. When a hiker in this physical condition first sees the summit, it is easy to fall into despair. We look at where we are and where we need to be, and we cannot fathom finding the ability to finish. Moments like this have sent many would-be climbers back down to their cars.

Knowing what she was thinking, I told her we needed to put our goal of reaching the summit aside for the moment and set up a series of small but manageable objectives.

I said, "See that big boulder at the bend in the trail about thirty yards up? Let's make it to that point and then rest. We can do that." And that was what we did. Then we chose another landmark and did it again. And again. We weren't just hikers that day. We were also learners—people who had to understand how to climb a mountain. We were students learning the slow art of what Nietzsche called "a long obedience in the same direction."[1]

Standing together at that trailhead was not unlike that day twenty years earlier when she and I had stood at the altar and made promises to each other that were bigger than either one of us. I didn't know it then, but when it came to our marriage I wasn't just learning how to be a husband, nor she just a wife. I was learning how to be *her* husband, and she was learning how to be *my* wife. Though this would certainly lead us to ways of relating common to any marriage, it would also forge between us a relationship as unique to this world as a fingerprint. And it would create experiences—small treks from one point to another—that would belong to the two of us that no one else would be able to fully share.

Let me describe it another way. Our marriage created an empty library, and we were two containers of books out at the curb, waiting to be brought in, cataloged, and shelved. In would come the stories we had been told, the books we had read, and the faith we had been given. In would come her history and in would come mine, along with her comedy and my drama and all of the mysteries that lie between a man and a woman.

After we brought in all we had, only a fraction of the shelves was filled. Those empty shelves were waiting for what was yet to be written. Slowly but surely, volumes of lamentation, praise, art, humor, geography, vocation, finance, education, home improvement, medicine, biblical studies, theology, grief, parenting, gardening, and inspiration would find their place among those stacks.

New characters would be introduced and other characters would leave. This, of course, is nothing new. Most of the roads good friends walk in life eventually diverge. There is nothing for it. We can have the closest of friendships for a season, but when a semester ends, or someone moves away, or circumstances change, we often find that our sense of closeness tapers off.

There is only one human relationship we come to know in this life that is meant by God to be intimate in affection, proximity, and purpose until death itself separates us—the marriage relationship. In marriage God gives a gift of incalculable worth—a sworn partner for life.

Lisa and I are like two tectonic plates who, by God's grace, grind away at each other's rough edges until we fuse together into a brand-new land. My nearsightedness and pride collide with her courage and wisdom. Her woundedness and fear run aground on the shores of my boyish optimism and confidence. And these collisions shape us both.

But when we stood hand in hand at the altar, promising to stay in this covenant for better or worse, in sickness and in health, until one of us died, we knew little of each other's worlds. Now, twenty years in, however, we know much more. With God as my witness we do.

I know how to make her laugh, and I know how to make her cry. I know how to feed her fear, and I know how to awaken her hope. I know what keeps her up and what gives her rest. I have the power to hurt her more deeply than anyone else on this planet, as she has with me. We have learned to speak in each other's native tongue and to see through one another's atmospheres down to the terra firma.

Yes, we see through a glass darkly, and we have much to learn. But we see so much more now than we could have ever imagined when we first took our vows.

I have fears that are known only to her and my Maker—not because I hide them from the rest of the world but because they are so nuanced and deep it would take someone who has been at my side for half of my life to know their triggers and to read them. There are qualities of beauty and fragility deep inside of her that no one else will ever know in the ways I do, though some I am seeing sprout up in the four children our God has given us. When I see my children carry my wife's beauty in them, I understand eternity in ways that never before occurred to me. Traces of who we are will remain long after we're gone.

Lord, have mercy.

Christ, have mercy.

Lord, have mercy.

As we climbed, we talked about the African proverb that says, "When an old man dies, a library burns to the ground," and how marriage is the holy curation of another person's life.

There are parts of us and our stories we will take to our graves—riches, wonders, inside jokes, sorrows, and prayers no one but she and I will ever know. And faults. There is no one in this world better acquainted with my faults than my wife. She could tell stories about my self-absorption, my impatience, my weaknesses, my inconsistencies, my fears, and my self-protective methods of containing them. She could talk about times I have chosen myself over her. She could recount instances when I have spoken angrily about people I have been called to love. She could go on and on about moments when I have behaved more like a child than an adult.

But after twenty years, here is what I have come to trust: she won't. Not without good reason. She won't complain about me to others. She won't saddle our children with her frustrations about their father. She will not try to forge new friendships by making jokes at my expense, no matter how lonely she feels. I trust she won't do these things because for twenty years this has been her way—never to speak ill of me to others.

This doesn't mean there are no ills of which to speak. There are plenty. We are human. And in cases where talking about our faults with others would help us move toward each other, we work at being willing to bring them to light.

There are faults in me—some subtle, others chronic—that most people will never know in the ways she does. By God's grace, she treats them as sacred. I am not crediting her with mere discretion. She counts the work of watching over my dignity and reputation as a holy calling—as part of the way she fulfills her vow to take me as her husband to love and to cherish, for better or worse, in sickness and in health, until death separates us.

This thought—that Lisa and I will enjoy a sort of life known only to one another—adds to the sanctity and beauty of our union. Though much of what she and I are will continue on in the lives of our kids, some of it will be buried when one of us dies. Not even our own children will fully grasp who this woman and I have become and are becoming to one another and to everyone else we know because of our relationship. Lord willing, each of my children will also take on this sort of union one day. And when they do, there will be many facets of their lives I will simply not have access to, nor should I.

This woman—my wife, standing just above the tree line, gasping for breath in the thin mountain air as she surveys the distant summit—is a marvel. In many ways, the rest of the world will have to take my word for it, because no one will ever know all that I know.

Nevertheless, if I'm being honest, when I see her struggling with the difficulty of this journey, I feel a pang of guilt. On account of me, she's having to dig deep.

We carried a lot up that mountain that day, she and I. We carried our physical limits and our fears of the unknown. She wondered if we would be able to do it. I knew we would because I had done it before, but I also knew it would involve making peace with a fair amount of pain and pushing well past the limits of what either of us were accustomed to during the course of a normal day.

This has been the story for the past two years. Our life together has been made up of a series of difficult but manageable objectives. Kill the bacteria. Operate on the heart. Convalesce. Battle depression. Take the drugs. Do the rehab. Process the emotions. Rebuild relationships. Bury a friend and grieve with her family. Express our sorrow to God. We have taken these things as they have come, certain that much more lies ahead.

She and I are not the same people we were when this all started. We have walked through the valley of the shadow of death.[2] We have received trouble from the hand of God.[3] We have asked God why, and the One who laid the foundations of the earth and determined its measurements, the One who commands the morning and causes the dawn to know its place, the One who walks in the recesses of the deep has declined, on many counts, to explain himself.[4]

What he has given us instead is help. He has given us love, joy, peace, patience, kindness, faithfulness, gentleness, goodness, and self-control.[5] Against these things there is no law. He has reminded us that when a son asks his father for bread, the father does not hand him a stone.[6] He has borne our griefs, carried our sorrows, and told us that by his wounds we are healed.[7] And he has given us faith to trust him.

He has also given us each other. One day death will separate us—this much is certain. But for now she is my traveling companion. We navigate this life by moving from one measurable objective to another, stopping to rest, waiting for one another, and pressing on toward a glorious end.

The Lord gives and the Lord takes away. Blessed be the name of the Lord.[8]

We reached the summit of Quandary Peak not by climbing a mountain but by moving from one boulder to another, and repeating that pattern again and again. Nothing about it was easy, but everything about it was doable.

I believe this is how we move through life—moving from one point to the next. There are no shortcuts to the end of the trail, but that is fine because the trail itself has a wonder and glory of its own. So we carry on, trusting that the path is leading us someplace good but also trying to pay attention to the beauty around us. When the way is hard, that can be tough to do.

From the top of the mountain we could see the trail we had taken—thin as a line from a pencil. We could see ascending hikers we had passed, and others who had passed us and were well on their way back down. We pointed out difficult sections with a hint of nostalgia, though we had been on them only a couple of hours earlier. We found the scary, steep boulder scramble that almost convinced us both to turn back, but from where we stood now it didn't look so bad. We tried to guess where we had started down below the tree line, but we couldn't be sure. That first part of the climb felt like it happened ages ago.

A few other hikers and a couple of unimpressed mountain goats met us at the top. We got a photo of the two of us standing together on the geological survey marker that identified the highest point. We had made it. By walking a collection of short routes with varying degrees of difficulty, we climbed to the top of a mountain.

Then we turned around and looked down over the other side of the summit. It looked steep and wild, unknown and untamed. Everything in me wanted to crest the ridge and go down the other side into the magnificent mystery of what seemed to stretch on forever—a world without end.[9] Something in its glory called to us, telling us we were made for more, beckoning us to go on and on and on.

I believe that in the end this is exactly what I will do.

CHAPTER 16

THE BIRD
AND THE BOY

A Doxology of Praise

*I must take care, on the one hand,
never to despise, or be ungrateful for,
these earthly blessings, and on the other,
never to mistake them for the something
else of which they are only a kind of copy,
or echo, or mirage. I must keep alive in
myself the desire for my true country,
which I shall not find till after death.*

C. S. LEWIS

Whathas come of my faith now that I am more like the bird
than the boy?

The man standing on the top of Quandary Peak has come a long
way from the boy with the bird in the Indiana snow. But my desire

to cross over the summit and keep going has its roots in the same longing that inspired me to raise that dead dove up to God and pray for its resurrection: belief in a power and glory that lies beyond what I have seen.

I have explored this terrain enough to know that the glory I long for will not be found on this side of the mountain. My time in the wild has taught me that this is a hard land and I am a man with limits. Yes, summit views are magnificent, but to reach them I must spend everything I have. Once I finally make it the top, I have to sit and collect myself for a while before I am physically ready to appreciate the accomplishment. And even when I have recovered enough to take in the view, in the back of my mind is the knowledge that I can't stay long, lest I find myself exposed on the summit when the afternoon thunderheads roll in.

I go through all that effort to make the climb to get a taste of glory, but the beauty before me is only an echo of the glory I seek. And I, with my physical limits, am only a fraction of the man I long to be. Still I climb because of this conviction I have about a glory I have not yet seen, but will.[1]

I didn't know how this journey would unfold back when my affliction began, and I cannot assume that any future season of suffering will follow the exact same course. But I can bear witness to what has come of my faith in this season of suffering.

Here is my confession. Through all of the pain, uncertainty, and grief, God's grace has been sufficient for me.[2] This grace is a gift, and so is the faith through which it comes—I cannot take credit for either.[3] But they are at work in me. I have not found the promises of God to be lacking. Out here beyond the limits of what I ever could have imagined, I find that they hold. Like the boy with the dove in his hands and a prayer on his lips, I believe them still. I really do.

If this sounds like a boast, I suppose it is. But I do not boast in myself. I boast in God's faithfulness, because I am neither smart enough nor tenacious enough to construct the sort of faith that has sustained me. Left to me, I would load it down with conditions, demands, and near-sighted expectations, and it would have collapsed by now under their weight. Of course I still worry about things beyond my control, but my faith has held. Fear has not defined this season.

What has? Longing.

But it is not a longing to be well, or strong, or in a more ideal situation in life. It is, as C. S. Lewis describes it, a longing not for better things but for the *best possible*. And that is a longing for something this world cannot deliver.[4] It is a longing for crying, death, sadness, tears, and pain to cease. It is a desire to live in perfect peace with our bodies, our friends, and our God. It is a longing for this world to be made new.[5]

What do we do with longings that nothing in this world can satisfy? Lewis says we can come at them in one of three ways—in the way of the fool, in the way of the disillusioned, or in the way of the Christian.

The fool naively assumes that every desire can and should be satisfied in this world. Perfection is out there, one just needs to find it. When the people, places, and things in life come up wanting, the fool blames them for not being better than they are. They are cut loose, one after another, until the longing for perfection is no longer compelling but boring, because even the best things in life have lost their shine.

The disillusioned concludes that the "best possible" is not available; pursuing it is chasing after the wind—a fool's errand. The disillusioned reduces desire to a matter of managing expectations. Happiness is not found in having your desires perfectly met, but rather by sensibly reducing them so they can be met by what is readily available. This is the sort of person Vincent van Gogh had in mind when he wrote to his brother Theo, "There exists in most men a poet who died young, whom the man survived."[6] To this, the disillusioned would add, "Yes, and the sooner that happens the better."

The Christian, however, assumes that we would not have the desires we do if there was no way for them to be satisfied. So if the deepest longings in my soul cannot be fulfilled in this world, then I must conclude that I was made for another. And if I physically lack the capacity to fully engage the glory that world will hold, then I should also expect that I, myself, must be renewed.

Unmet desires in this life are intended to arouse a hunger for the next. Physical limitations are felt as an ache for a perfected body.[7] Coming face to face with my mortality has awakened my appetite for eternity. As I have stood at the summit and surveyed the distant mountains beyond, I have longed to explore. Beyond what I can see lies a glory I know I was made to behold. The grand adventure tugs at my heart, and one day I will go.

But today is not that day. I am grateful that the path the Lord has for me now is one that has brought me home to my family and community. I love these people, and I love this place. May the Lord continually teach me how to be present in this life for as long as I draw breath.

~~~~

Everyone I know is either in the middle of a season of struggle, just coming out of one, or soon to go into one. For some, all three are true. Where are you in your climb? Maybe you are in the early steps and are not even winded yet. Or maybe you are deep in the woods with no sight of the summit, trudging on with little sense of purpose or progress, bone tired and discouraged. Or perhaps you have emerged from the thick of things and have caught a glimpse of the distant peak, and you feel your strength returning.

Maybe you're watching someone you love struggle, and you hurt because you can walk with them only so far, but then no further. Maybe even now you're watching as a loved one crests a certain final ridge, and you know it is not your time to follow.

Or perhaps you are the one who has crossed over, and you know you must walk this part alone to its end as those who love you look on.

Tim Keller wrote, "Human beings are hope-shaped creatures. The way you live now is completely controlled by what you believe about the future."[8] My prayer for you is that your struggles and afflictions would be filled with the hope that all the pain will one day end.

This isn't a hope we can create or muster. It must be given. And by the grace of God it is—a hope that "does not put us to shame, because God's love has been poured into our hearts through the Holy Spirit who has been given to us. For while we were still weak, at the right time Christ died for the ungodly."[9]

———

This is what my hope looks like.

I believe that the day will come when the Maker of heaven and earth will scoop me up, all cold and still, and warm my spirit to flight. I will rise up and ascend to heights of a glory unknown though thoroughly familiar. All of my infirmities will be removed and my sorrows comforted. All of my anger, impatience, fear, pride, greed, envy, and lust will fall off like dragon scales, but I will neither tire nor fall.

I will pass through a great gathering of saints—a cloud of witnesses each shaped in some way by the collision of affliction and faith. I will see the flawed heroes I have known only through the pages of Scripture—King David, Simon Peter, Abraham and Sarah, the apostle Paul. I will see Alice and Barbara and countless others I have loved who will have gone on before me. I wonder what that will be like. Maybe even the man in the mask will show his face.

Here is what I do know. I will be at peace in the presence of my God, who raised from the dead his Son Jesus Christ, whose blood bought my freedom, whose triumph over the grave guaranteed my healing, and in whose name I have eternal life.[10] With clear eyes I will see the Author and Perfecter of my faith seated at the right hand of the Father, robed in the authority I struggled to accept, in the power I failed to trust, in the wisdom I could not understand, and in the beauty I was unable to imagine. He will receive me with the joy for which he endured the cross and scorned its shame.[11] My healer. My shepherd. My king. My God.

Held aloft on the waves of the peals of a bell struck before the foundation of the world, I will go on and on and on.[12] And I will say at last to the glory laid out before me, "Oh, there you are."

*Wait but a little while, my soul, wait
for the Divine promise, and thou shalt have
abundance of all good things in heaven.*

THOMAS À KEMPIS

*Come to me, all who labor and are
heavy laden, and I will give you rest.*

MATTHEW 11:28

AFTERWORD

A Wife's Response to
Her Husband's Affliction

Lisa Ramsey

Suck it up."

This expression has become a joke between us now, but by the second week of Russ's fever this was the sum total of my sympathy. I am telling you this because he will only tell you positive things about me.

Russ didn't sit around moping about not feeling well. He had taken a round of antibiotics that had not helped. But he was still going to work and staying busy, so it didn't seem like whatever was wrong with him could be that bad.

All of this happened in May, which for a mom is one of the craziest months of the year. As a part-time teacher and full-time parent of four students, life was very busy. End-of-the-year concerts, school award programs, carpools, and appreciation weeks filled all of our schedules to the rim. So my counsel was, "Suck it up. Or go to the doctor. Let me know how it goes."

On the Tuesday when his doctor told him to go to the ER, Russ called my cell and told me where he was headed. We were still under the impression that he was just going to need IV antibiotics or fluids and that this wasn't a big deal—worse than the random virus, but still easily fixed.

I shuttled the kids home from their schools, quickly ran through homework and dinner, and then headed to the hospital to see how Russ was doing. He was still in the ER waiting for a room. As I was passing through security, a gunshot victim was dropped off at the curb and the ER went into lockdown. I was stuck in the waiting room for almost two hours before I could see him.

As I waited, our friend Tim—who is a physician at the hospital—came to see me. Tim wanted me to know that Russ was okay. Sympathetically, he told me not to worry. At this point I didn't know I was supposed to be worried, so I was confused. He then proceeded to tell me that Russ had an allergic reaction to penicillin, but they were able to stabilize him and he was fine now. Russ had never had an allergic reaction to medicine before. I have some severe allergies, so I knew what Tim was saying was bad.

When I did finally get back to see Russ, he was pretty weak and out of it. Because of the lockdown it was late by the time I got to him. I couldn't stay long. I had to get back home to take care of kids and keep the routine going for another day.

A couple days later, Russ was feeling better and ready for the kids to come visit him at the hospital. He had been run through numerous tests and tons of blood work but was also getting good medication that seemed to be helping. Things were looking up, and we assumed he would be coming home at any point.

When we got to Russ's room, the kids ran in ahead of me just as a team of doctors were leaving. Our friend Tim (an incredible gift to us who served as a medical translator for me throughout the entire process) stopped me in the hallway and proceeded to explain what the surgical team had just told my husband.

As I half listened, I looked into the room right as Russ burst into tears. The kids began crying too. They didn't know what was happening, but Russ was still processing the news that he would need open-heart surgery as soon as possible.

I let the kids get in their hugs and questions, and then rounded them up to get them home. After homework and dinner, I got the kids in bed and headed back to the hospital to begin processing with Russ what was going to happen next.

The rest of Russ's hospitalization that week was about healing the infection. Nothing else could happen until they had that under control. I tried to keep our home routine as "normal" as I could so the kids would feel stable. Their teachers were so gracious with us as we stumbled our way through the final days of the school year. The friends and family who helped watch our kids while we went to the hospital for tests and doctor visits gave us just enough bandwidth to keep going.

For me, doing practical daily activities was a way to keep moving forward. I was not processing a lot of emotion, and honestly, I did not want to. I could hold it together if I stayed with my checklists.

Then one day on the way to the hospital, I called a sweet friend from Kansas. When she answered the phone neither of us could talk. I just cried, and she cried with me. That might have been the most therapeutic five minutes in the week. What a gift to not have to say a word and just have someone grieve with you—especially when you are not aware that you need to grieve.

Russ was discharged with a fanny pack that contained a small machine that pumped meds. (He was really excited about that fanny pack. Not kidding.) After a month of IV antibiotics, his blood was clean. He was ready for surgery.

On the day of surgery, we drove to the hospital before dawn. When we arrived, our friend Eric was waiting for us in the lobby. He and Russ went to seminary together, and now he was pastoring a church in our town. He came to pray over us and to pray for the surgery. I didn't know he would be there. It was a blessing to have someone pray over the day with us, and it was especially powerful for me. For the past few weeks I had been moving forward through our routines. But now I had to stop and be prayed for. I had been praying, but Russ had been the needy one. Eric's prayer was a reminder that I was needy as well. I was no more in control of the situation than anyone else in the waiting room. My checklists and routines had reached their limits of usefulness, and my helplessness was consuming. All I could do was rest in the sovereignty of God and trust his love for me, for Russ, and for our family.

I went to the pre-op waiting room. This was where "significant others" stayed while their loved ones got checked in (and shaved, I guess). Once the patient was prepped for surgery, we were permitted to go in to see them one more time before they went under.

In the pre-op waiting room, I met a woman who was the worst Debbie Downer you can imagine. She went around to each person in the room, asking us why we were there. In every case, she had horrible statistics or thoughts for each of us. After she did this with 4 or 5 people, it became comical. I was amazed at some of the stories people were willing to tell her about their journeys.

Some of the details people offered this woman made our situation seem almost routine. One of the takeaways from this season for me was being able to experience the hospital culture for long-term patients. We met so many people who were not local and hadn't been able to see family in months for fear of illness or infection. It was amazing and humbling.

While Russ was in the hospital and I was putting many miles on the car driving back and forth between there and home, I would feel so removed from "normal" life. I wondered how many others felt the same. How many people around me were walking through incredible life-changing events? Not just bad days. Tectonic shifts. I needed so much more compassion and far greater mercy.

***

After I watched Russ get wheeled away to surgery, I headed back down to the main lobby where I would watch the screen scroll through updates. Eric was still there. Though I hadn't thought to have a friend there with me, it was a blessing to have someone to chat with as I started the long wait. He eventually had to go, so he sent his wife, Jenn, to spend the rest of the day with me.

Jenn had not planned on doing this and had to rearrange her schedule to make it happen. But she did, and I cannot thank her enough for being there. A few people stopped by to check on us, and I received a lot of text messages, but having a friend present with me all day was a fantastic gift.

Russ's parents were gracious enough to stay home with the kids through the morning, and I was grateful that the kids had family with them while they waited. That afternoon, some kind friends, Brad and Amy Katherine, came to the house and brought their dogs, which occupied the kids while Russ's folks came up to the hospital for the end of surgery.

It is a holy service to take care of someone's kids during a crisis. In times like these, none of us are at our best. Trusting someone to handle our brokenness and chaos, and love us anyway, is really hard. I am so thankful for the people who helped make it easier during this time.

I know I am mentioning a lot of people, but I think it is helpful to see how many it takes to walk a family through a crisis. For us, it was not the same people all of the time. Please let that be an encouragement to anyone who has the opportunity to help be the church for some person or family in need. If I could, I would list every single person who brought us food. And I couldn't even begin to name all those who prayed, or the number of times people did things for us without our asking. This was so valuable because if someone called and asked what we needed, most of the time I really couldn't answer them. Often, I didn't know. I could only deal with what was in front of me.

One day I came home to our riding mower up on blocks with the blades missing. Someone mowed our yard and then took the blades to sharpen them. Another time, my sweet friend Susan showed up at the hospital, handed me Starbucks, and then turned around and left. She stayed all of five minutes, but that gesture kept me going for the whole day.

In the waiting area, there was a phone that the operating room would call when they had updates. The first update on Russ came a few hours into surgery. They had been able to repair the valve and did not have to replace it. He was doing well. The second was when they were finishing and getting ready to send him to recovery. After that call, we were moved to a different room to wait for the doctors, who would take us to see Russ.

When we were finally able to see him in the cardiovascular ICU, he was still out of it. Eventually, the anesthesia began to wear off and he started to come to. My daughter's teacher warned me before surgery that he would look bad (her husband had the same surgery), and she was right. He was hooked up to a lot of machines. Tubes flowed from just about every part of his body. But he was alive.

Over the next twenty-four hours, they pulled the tubes out one by one. The cardiac nurses were amazing, and their steadiness convinced us that everything was going just as it should.

But there was a problem. Russ's mom noticed it first. His left foot was rolled over to the side, limp. We knew regaining speech would be an issue because of all the drugs and tubes, but he could not move his foot. He had experienced something the doctors would only refer to as a "neurological event" that left his foot paralyzed.

Thankfully, sensation in his foot slowly returned. By the time they moved him to the step-down room, he was able to drag it forward with his leg. But we realized through his speech that his brain was not communicating like it should. Little things were misfiring, like saying yes when he meant no and not remembering where I was.

I had planned to run home in the evenings while his mom was there so I could shower, tuck kids in, and get a bite to eat. But if I went out of the room for more than five minutes, Russ panicked because he didn't know where I was. I would tell him where I was going, but he would have no recollection of the conversation. He was frustrated and angry because the dots were not connecting in his mind. So most of the time I just stayed.

The kids came to see him, to much greater success than that first visit. I did not have the brain space to think about food, so I walked downstairs to the same restaurant every day and got the same meal—a bagel or a cup of fruit. I was not too interested in what I was eating.

By Friday, Russ was finally getting around on his own with a walking boot. We did laps around the little hallway as he built up strength. We watched old sitcoms and laughed hilariously at dumb jokes. Russ crushed every neurological test they threw his way. Each day, he seemed to get exponentially better.

When you are in the hospital, progress from one day to the next can seem huge. You can feel like you are getting back to normal, or in Russ's case better than normal since the fever was gone. But then you go home, and you discover that "hospital normal" and "real-life normal" are two different things.

Russ could not be left alone at all for the first four weeks. It was summertime. The kids were troopers about it, but that changed our lifestyle. Driving Russ for physical therapy appointments and follow-up doctor visits became part of the routine.

Just as the kids were getting back into their school routines and Russ was starting to get his sea legs back, he started having chest pains and ended up back in the hospital because of an inflammation in the lining of his heart. Typically, this is not something that requires hospitalization, but due to his recent surgery they needed to be sure there was no infection. Our hospital routine began again, but thankfully only lasted a week.

As Russ recovered and continued to regain strength, he was released to drive and resume some partial work responsibilities. When this happened, I almost forgot the extent of the trauma of the last few months. I dealt with so much of this season of affliction through routines. When my routines were "on," life was manageable. But when I would see the scar on Russ's chest, it would remind me what we had been through. As the urgency of the season wore off and space opened for me to begin thinking about the past weeks and months, I realized that I had lost a lot of myself.

As a mom, there is a great big portion of myself that is defined by family. I am my children's mother. I am Russ's wife. But when I became "Russ the Afflicted's" wife, I became the lady with the updates. I was the gateway to finding out information about Russ.

To clarify, I did not mind this role. It fell neatly into my list of routines, and I was very happy to do it. What it did though, over time, was allow me to hide behind the information. Plenty of people would ask me how I was doing, but I didn't know. I just knew Russ's updates, his stats. That was a safe place to hide. People did not expect me to give much beyond that.

I felt plenty of positive emotions: relief that Russ had made it through surgery, gratitude for our community group and all of the people who had loved us so well through his days in the hospital, optimism that this was a one-time deal. But there was plenty to grieve from the hospital season as well. It is so hard to grieve when you are happy, but I needed to grieve to make peace with the other emotions. I needed to remember the intense fear and anger and loss I felt during that season. I may have been able to cover them with busyness, but those emotions still existed.

God has given me a couple of friends who know me well enough to sit and let me process what I'm thinking without judgment—the fear of losing Russ and our family as we knew it, the loss of a summer of carefree rest, the anger that God would not handle the details as I thought he should. I needed this, because sometimes anger, hurt, sadness, and frustration can overwhelm me without warning. It is a special person who can lovingly walk with me through that fear, hurt, sadness, frustration and even anger at my spouse (yes, the one *recovering from open-heart surgery*) and then see through to my heart and know that I am anxious and afraid.

Friends like these are precious. Several years ago, God assembled a group of women who spent years growing children together. We celebrated each other's highs and wept over one another's lows. I believe he did this for me and our open-heart season. (They will probably tell you it was about them—don't believe them.) Those years of established relationship gave me a safe place to be vulnerable and grieve.

I know life is busy, but I encourage you to invest in relationships. Let people share in your mess and let them share their mess with you as well. If you struggle to find that friend, pray for one and ask God to open your eyes to someone who might need you as well. I believe he loves to provide these relationships.

I am writing these words almost two years after Russ's surgery and illness. Recently, I was studying Ecclesiastes and thinking about the comparison of life on earth to life eternal. Where I place my focus greatly impacts how I live my life and what I fear.

I once heard Tim Keller describe the fear of God as "wonderfilled bold humility." When I compare my fears about this life and my fear of God, I do not want to be someone who fears what is only temporary. I want to keep my focus and fear placed firmly on my Creator. While circumstances in this life can certainly cause fear and worry, I am comforted by the fierceness of his love for me. As the apostle Paul tells us, "No, in all these things we are more than conquerors through him who loved us. For I am sure that neither death nor life, nor angels nor rulers, nor things present nor things to come, nor powers, nor height nor depth, nor anything else in all creation, will be able to separate us from the love of God in Christ Jesus our Lord."[1]

I do not have a big lesson to share with you about what God taught me while we were going through this season. I often wish I had. I would love to be able to tie a neat bow around those months and say I learned what I was supposed to learn—checklist complete—or to feel like a completely different, spiritual giant who has faced my husband's mortality and can now face life without fear and worry.

Unfortunately, I can't. I know I am changed for the experience. I have learned that I am a far needier person than I give myself credit for, and that God cares for me in better ways than I could have imagined.

I am thankful for the way God has sustained us through this season, and I am overwhelmed by his mercy. He knew what I needed when I needed it when I did not even know how to ask or pray. He has molded and shaped my heart even when I have tried to bury it in layers of routine and denial. He has carried me and shown me my greater need for him.

I thought I was doing a pretty great job of hiding. But I was not hidden from him. And neither are you.

ACKNOWLEDGMENTS

For their support, encouragement, inspiration, and in some cases, life-saving skills, I wish to thank the following:

Lisa, Chris, Margaret, Kate, and Jane.

Rick and Susan Ramsey, Ryan and Nancy Ramsey, and Nathan and A. J. Durham.

Dr. Jason Periera, Dr. Rashid Ahmed, Dr. Timothy Girard, Dr. Tiffany Alexander, and the entire team at Vanderbilt Medical Center.

Travis and Rachel Keller, Rick and Laura Pierce, and Scott and Patti Sauls.

John Ambrose, Shelley Ellis, Roy and Rachel Roper, Jonathan and Lou Alice Rogers, John and Lisa Harrison, Drew and Susan Trotman, and Locke and Cynthia Sandahl.

Winn Elliott, Jeremy Casella, Nick Pilkington, Andrew Peterson, A. S. Peterson, Doug McKelvey, Andrew Osenga, Amanda Williams, Raechel Myers, Claire Gibson, Barnabas Piper, Korey Pollard, and Daniel and Samantha Fisher.

Annie Dillard, C. S. Lewis, Timothy Keller, Cormac McCarthy, Leif Enger, and E. B. White.

Al Hsu and the entire team at IVP.

And special thanks to Andrew Wolgemuth.

NOTES

1 LEARNING TO SEE: AFFLICTION AND FAITH

[1]Annie Dillard, *Pilgrim at Tinker Creek* (New York: Harper & Row, 1985), 25.

[2]Ibid., 28.

[3]Ibid., 26-27.

[4]Ibid., 29.

[5]Ibid., 36.

[6]Ibid., 30.

2 STRUCK: THE ONSET OF AFFLICTION

[1]Matthew 6:26.

[2]Matthew 10:30.

[3]Psalm 139:14.

[4]Psalm 24:1.

[5]Luke 7:1-10.

[6]John 6:40.

[7]1 Corinthians 15:12-49.

[8]Romans 8:20-25.

[9]C. S. Lewis, *Mere Christianity* (Glasgow: Collins, 1952), 118.

[10]N. T. Wright, *Surprised by Hope: Rethinking Heaven, the Resurrection, and the Mission of the Church* (New York: Harper One, 2008), 108.

3 THE SACRAMENTAL ECHO: DIAGNOSIS

[1]Mark 4:26-27.

[2]Isaiah 64:4.

[3]Psalm 139.

[4]Hebrews 10:31.

[5]This quote, which is the title of a book on the Psalms of Ascent by Eugene Peterson, comes from the atheist philosopher Friedrich Nietzsche, who said, "The essential thing 'in heaven and earth' is . . . that there should be long obedience in the same direction; there thereby results, and has always resulted in the long run, something which has made life worth living." As quoted in Eugene Peterson, *A Long Obedience in the Same Direction* (Downers Grove, IL: InterVarsity Press, 2000), 17.

[6]John 10:10.

5 THE DISTANCE: THE SPACE BETWEEN THE SICK AND THE WELL

[1]Luke 22:42.

[2]Job 13:15.

[3]Isaiah 55:8.

[4]Hebrews 11:1.

6 THE LETTERS: PUTTING A HOUSE IN ORDER

[1]1 Corinthians 4:1-5.

[2]Ecclesiastes 7:14 (NIV).

[3]Job 2:10.

[4]1 Corinthians 13:12.

[5]Isaiah 55:9.

[6]Job 40:2.

[7]Isaiah 53:4.

[8]Romans 5:9.

[9]Acts 17:28.

[10]Job 1:21.

7 SCOWLING AT THE ANGEL: SURGERY AND WAKING UP

[1]Matthew 28:1-10.

[2]Genesis 18:1-15.

[3]John 21:18.

[4]Exodus 34:29-30.

[5]Proverbs 15:1.

[6]Proverbs 31:26.

[7]Galatians 5:22-23.

8 Scar Tissue: Physical Healing and Resiliency

[1]Romans 6:23.
[2]Genesis 2:17; Romans 5:12.
[3]1 Corinthians 15:50-58.
[4]Genesis 1:27.
[5]John 11:17-27.

9 Monster in the Dark: Depression

[1]Annie Dillard, *The Writing Life* (New York: Harper Perennial, 1989), 32.

11 A Tornado in a Trailer Park: Anger and Ego

[1]Galatians 6:2, John 15:13.
[2]Genesis 11:1-9.
[3]1 Corinthians 1:19.
[4]Psalm 23.
[5]Job 2:10.
[6]Hebrews 11:1.
[7]Job 1:21.
[8]Sheldon Vanauken, *A Severe Mercy* (New York: Harper Collins, 1977).

12 Seeing with Clearer Eyes: Recognizing the Need to Lament

[1]See Psalm 71 for an example of a biblical lament. It opens by addressing God (vv. 1-3), followed by a complaint (v. 4). The complaint is followed by a confession of trust (vv. 5-8), which is followed by an appeal for God's intervention (vv. 9-13). The lament ends with words of assurance (v. 14) and a vow to praise God no matter what happens (vv. 15-24).

[2]Throughout this chapter, I have depended on and am grateful for Dr. Jaco Hamman's book *When Steeples Cry: Leading Congregations Through Loss and Change* (Cleveland: Pilgrim Press, 2005). I have freely borrowed and incorporated, with his permission, many of his insights concerning the process and art of lament into this section. Specifically, I have drawn on his insights concerning the importance and power of lament, the difference between grief and mourning, the types of loss, and the structure of a biblical lament.

13 BARBARA: RETURNING TO THE WORK OF BURDEN BEARING

[1]John 1:1-5.
[2]John 1:29.
[3]John 2:1-11.
[4]John 3:16.
[5]John 4.
[6]John 5:6.
[7]John 6:22-71.
[8]C. S. Lewis, *A Grief Observed* (San Francisco: Harper Collins, 1994), 63.

14 A SONG OF LAMENT: A YEAR OF GRAPPLING WITH SUFFERING BEFORE GOD

[1]1 Peter 4:17-19.
[2]Isaiah 43:5; Psalm 23.
[3]Psalm 23.
[4]Genesis 21:16.
[5]2 Samuel 11:14-21.
[6]Matthew 26:74-75.
[7]Hebrews 10:31.
[8]Psalm 69:2; 73:2.
[9]Psalm 77:3.
[10]Isaiah 42:3.
[11]Psalm 147:3.
[12]C. S. Lewis, *A Grief Observed* (San Francisco: Harper Collins, 1994), 69.
[13]John 6:68.
[14]John 21.
[15]2 Corinthians 12:9.
[16]1 Thessalonians 5:24.
[17]Genesis 1:31.
[18]Psalm 23.
[19]Romans 12:1.
[20]Jeremiah 31:13.
[21]Psalm 30:11.
[22]Psalm 19:14.

15 TO CLIMB A MOUNTAIN: FINDING A WAY FORWARD

[1]Eugene Peterson, *A Long Obedience in the Same Direction* (Downers Grove, IL: InterVarsity Press, 2000).

[2]Psalm 23.
[3]Job 2:10.
[4]Job 38–39.
[5]Galatians 5:22-23.
[6]Matthew 7:9-10.
[7]Isaiah 53:4-6.
[8]Job 1:21.
[9]Ephesians 3:21 (KJV).

16 THE BIRD AND THE BOY: A DOXOLOGY OF PRAISE

[1]Hebrews 11:1.
[2]2 Corinthians 12:9.
[3]Ephesians 2:8.
[4]This section about the three ways of longing relies heavily upon C. S. Lewis's words and structure from his chapter called "Hope" in *Mere Christianity* (Glasgow: Collins, 1952), 116-19. Here I elaborate, but the core ideas and a fair measure of the terminology belongs to him.
[5]Revelation 21:1-5.
[6]This quote, taken from a letter Vincent van Gogh wrote to his brother Theo (Paris, 15 July 1875), is Vincent's paraphrase of the French poet Charles Augustin Sainte-Beuve, who wrote, "In all of us, if we are poets, and even if we clearly are not, there exists or there has existed some fine flower of feelings, of desires, some primal dream, which soon vanishes into humdrum works and expires in the course of life's business. It is found, in a word, in three-quarters of mankind, like a poet who dies young, while the man lives on" (Charles Augustin Sainte-Beuve, *Revue des Deux Mondes*, April–June 1837, 645-46).
[7]Philippians 3:20-21.
[8]Tim Keller, *Walking with God Through Pain and Suffering* (New York: Dutton, 2013), 314.
[9]Romans 5:5-6.
[10]Hebrews 13:20-21.
[11]Hebrews 12:1-2.
[12]Ephesians 1:4.

AFTERWORD

[1]Romans 8:37-39.

ALSO AVAILABLE

Songs from Struck

Original songs by Russ Ramsey, thematically inspired by the events described in *Struck*.

"Dance with Me" is the song mentioned in chapter 6, "The Letters." Russ's vocal for this song was recorded only days before his surgery.

"The Ballad of Andy Catlett" is inspired by Wendell Berry's short novel *Remembering*, which explores themes of anger and forgiveness discussed in chapter 11, "A Tornado in a Trailer Park."

"Both Alive" (cowritten with Andrew Osenga, the friend who held Russ's letters to his family) tells a story based on themes discussed in chapter 5, "The Distance."

Available on iTunes and Spotify.